THE PURPOSE
of EDUCATION

THE PURPOSE
of EDUCATION

An EXAMINATION *of* EDUCATIONAL
PROBLEMS *in the* LIGHT *of* RECENT
SCIENTIFIC RESEARCH

by

ST GEORGE LANE FOX PITT

NEW CHEAP EDITION
REVISED & ENLARGED

CAMBRIDGE
at the
UNIVERSITY PRESS
MCMXXIV

CAMBRIDGE
UNIVERSITY PRESS

University Printing House, Cambridge CB2 8BS, United Kingdom

Cambridge University Press is part of the University of Cambridge.

It furthers the University's mission by disseminating knowledge in the pursuit of education, learning and research at the highest international levels of excellence.

www.cambridge.org
Information on this title: www.cambridge.org/9781316601655

First edition 1913
Second edition 1916
Reprinted 1919
Revised edition 1924
First paperback edition 2015

A catalogue record for this publication is available from the British Library

ISBN 978-1-316-60165-5 Paperback

PREFACE TO REVISED EDITION

SINCE the publication of the first edition in 1913, *The Purpose of Education* has provoked a good deal of discussion and criticism, which has been, for the most part, very instructive and helpful. The critics, although expressing themselves, on the whole, favourably, often asked for an expansion of the theme in certain directions, with a view to greater clearness. The last two editions appeared with an appendix, in which an attempt was made to meet this request. The substance of this appendix, together with some further additions, is now embodied in the text.

The main contention of the book remains the same. It is pointed out, and argued throughout, that both as to aim and method, modern education is often faulty in that the excessive desire shown to obtain tangible results of a practical nature has had the effect of obscuring its ideals and perverting its methods. Thus ideals have become confused, and in many cases "inverted." By "inversion" is meant that mental process that makes us see our interests, or relationships, upside down and inside out. In this edition a new chapter has been added dealing specifically with psychological inversion.

Many educationalists have insisted that they do not see their way to dispensing with competition as an incentive to effort, although they do at the same time recognise its drawbacks. They forget, however, that ill directed effort is effort wasted, or worse. Competition in education tends to engender in its votaries other qualities besides those they seek to evoke. Knowledge, skill and efficiency can indeed be acquired through competition, but a mental attitude is incidentally fostered which makes the competitor think his merits depend on those of his fellow competitors, and a desire arises to obtain superiority and supremacy over them.

Thus the tendency of competition is to make those engaged in it rejoice in the comparative inferiority of others. This vicious effect may no doubt be corrected in after years, but the poison remains in the system, and is hard to eradicate.

How then can we induce in the young a pure love of learning, and so develop and cultivate it that it may grow fruitfully? To speak of evil and wickedness does not really help us at all. A teacher can inspire the love of learning if he has it himself, and few are without the germs of this love. It is not enough that a teacher should be clever and learned. He must have a genuine enthusiasm for his calling, if he is to be really successful in making his pupils love learning for its own sake, or rather for the sake of its ennobling effect on their characters. A wise teacher would himself see and appreciate the truth that the securing of a relatively good reputation is a paltry achievement when contrasted with success in awakening in the young mind that true insight and love of right which triumphantly leads along the road towards perfection. That a high reputation would accompany this nobler development, though quite probable, should be regarded as comparatively unimportant. A generation of clever and learned rascals would soon bring a nation to ruin. It is sometimes laid down as an axiom that "education is the art of making people at home in their environment." Translated into current phraseology this dictum means that the purpose of education is to gain the power of "making money" or of keeping it; because commercialism certainly represents the dominant characteristic of the present day "environment." Now what does the "making of money" imply? It implies the exercise of a capacity for working selfishly (i.e., for a *legal consideration*) to gratify, or to forestall, the selfish wants of others. There need not necessarily be anything wrong in doing this, but can it be called a noble ideal?

The Science of Economics, if science it may be called, deals with "Wealth," its production, application and distribution.

Now *wealth*, in its strictly economical signification, is unmeaning apart from *property* and *market values*, for clearly there would be no distribution of wealth, whereby it changes hands, without the tacit recognition of ownership and the "rights of disposition." When, then, we speak of economic laws we must assume the existence of laws of contract and private property. These laws have developed slowly out of custom, tradition, practical expediency and a sense of justice. This last concept of *justice* is often supposed to have a very special moral and spiritual significance, although, as a fact, it is expressed through laws and customs in an arbitrary, contradictory and confused fashion, varying according to individual tastes and predilections. It was assumed, at one time, that this concept was of so fundamental and sacred a character that it must have existed from all eternity apart altogether from human nature. Indeed this assumption had become so dogmatic and was so deeply rooted in current thought, that many years ago John Stuart Mill took great pains to expose its falsity. The concept of justice has grown, like all other concepts, out of experience; and its value depends on its adaptability to human needs.

To the oft-repeated insistence that the economic side of life is very important, the answer is clear. Yes, certainly it is important, but it is not all-important. The true importance of the economic side of life lies in the just recognition of the fact that it is an artificial instrument of our social welfare, not an end in itself. It is an instrument for facilitating our co-operative activities in the direction of furnishing our material needs, and in maintaining or improving our mutual relations in peaceful fellowship. Human nature, as at present constituted, makes co-operation difficult in practice, without the means of exchanging wants and interests. It is indeed not often practicable for individuals, of varying capacities and talents, to work together spontaneously and without personal "consideration," for their mutual good. Our notions and feelings as to our respective interests or merits, being too narrow and circumscribed, too much charged with prejudice, are apt to clash with one another, unless we can devise some mutually acceptable mechanism to act as an efficient means of adjusting and controlling them. Hence the evolution of economic systems.

Now while it is important that we should understand and appreciate the working of these systems in their proper spheres of activity, it is no less important to see clearly their limitations, and to be mindful of their legitimate functions in relation to our higher welfare. It is the neglect of this precaution that gives rise to the evils of corruption and bribery. For as a fact we are of necessity *interdependent*. The belief in our individual *independence*, except as possessors of that inestimably precious power within ourselves whereby we are enabled to avoid the temptation of falling under the influence of pernicious suggestions and except in so far as we can develop individual initiative and self-control, is no more than a delusion and a snare.

These are things we all have to learn sooner or later, and we cannot begin to learn them too soon. The teacher, moreover, should not only know that, as a fact, these things are true; he should learn also to know how and why they are true. He should learn how and why beliefs, wishes and memories are related to one another, why they fluctuate, mingle and conflict. He should learn how and why our outlook upon life is so narrow and superficial; and above all he should learn to know the true remedy for this pettiness, and he should love to apply that remedy.

Of recent years we have witnessed, in various directions, a strong revolt against what is vaguely called the "mechanistic theory" of life, and against the "pernicious trend of materialistic science." This revolt is leading to an unholy revival of superstition and quackery on the one hand, and on the other to serious efforts to interpret the unexplained phenomena of life and mind by the evolution of the science of psycho-physical biology. This science although by no means new, has not yet received the attention it deserves. It does not require that all the laborious researches of eminent experimentalists in the fields of physics, physiology, chemistry, biology, psychology and anthropology should be discarded as useless, but it does require that the outcome of all these researches should be correlated and synthesised.

This small volume is intended to introduce inquirers to the elements of this science; and it is hoped that the psycho-physical treatment of educational problems may offer at least a clue to their satisfactory solution.

ST G. L. F. P.

TRAVELLERS' CLUB,
    LONDON, 1924.

This very interesting letter, from the late Professor Émile Boutroux de l'Académie française, was written in 1916, when a second edition of the book was in preparation.

LETTRE-PRÉFACE

Cher Monsieur,

Pardonnez-moi si, dans la crise présente, je ne trouve pas la liberté d'esprit et le loisir nécessaires pour réfléchir, comme je le souhaiterais, sur les graves enseignements contenus dans votre livre, auquel on pourrait appliquer le mot d'Aristote: καὶ τῷ ὄγκῳ μικρόν, δυνάμει καὶ τιμιότητι ὑπερέχει: "petit quant au volume, grand quant à l'importance et à la valeur."

Voici, entre autres, un point que j'eusse aimé approfondir, en suivant les directions que votre livre nous donne si nettement, et, à mon sens, si judicieusement.

L'homme qui s'interroge sur le sens dans lequel il doit orienter sa vie, pour remplir sa destinée d'homme, aperçoit devant lui deux voies opposées, dont chacune se donne pour la voie unique et véritable: l'une va du dedans au dehors, de l'homme aux choses, de l'esprit à la nature; l'autre va de la nature à l'esprit, du milieu environnant à la conscience, des choses à l'homme. Deux partis, disait Horace, s'offrent à moi: *mihi res, aut me rebus subjungere.*

Cette éternelle alternative devint, au siècle dernier, le conflit de la religion et de la science, comme directrices de la vie humaine. Selon les avocats de la science, la sagesse consiste dans l'adaptation pure et simple du dedans au dehors, c'est-à-dire de l'homme à son milieu, tel que nous le fait connaître une observation strictement objective. Selon les avocats de la religion, l'esprit échappe aux étreintes de la science, et trouve, dans son attache au créateur, toutes les conditions de sa vie propre.

On ne saurait nier que, dans la seconde moitié du siècle dernier, les allures du scientisme ne fussent devenues de plus en plus triomphantes. La science envahissait, peu à peu, tous les domaines qui avaient paru lui être à jamais interdits : la vie, l'âme, la société, l'art, la morale, la religion même. Or, si, effectivement, tout ce qui est ou peut être, sans aucune exception, ressortissait à la science et, par conséquent, était soumis, littéralement, au déterminisme scientifique, quel autre objet pourrait se proposer la culture humaine, sinon de former l'homme au genre de vie que lui assigne, selon les données de la science, le milieu où la nature l'a placé ?

A beaucoup d'esprits la victoire du scientisme sembla définitive. La religion, la morale, à leur gré, n'avaient de réalité qu'en tant que branches de l'histoire naturelle.

Mais, depuis un certain temps, cette conception purement objective des choses est fort discutée. On a mis en valeur le rôle de l'instinct, comme irréductible à cette connaissance abstraite et raisonnée, dont la science positive est la forme perfectionnée. On a observé que l'instinct ne guide pas seulement, de la manière la plus utile, notre vie physique, mais qu'il nous fournit les suggestions les plus hautes et les impulsions les plus généreuses, dans le domaine de la vie morale et religieuse elle-même.

L'instinct, dès lors, ne serait-il pas comme la perception directe et vivante de l'être, tandis que la science opérerait, non sur l'être lui-même, mais sur des symboles artificiels, appropriés à notre imagination et à notre entendement ?

C'est, d'une manière générale, le caractère des spéculations de ces derniers temps, d'avoir, en tout domaine, restitué la valeur de l'instinct ou de l'intuition, c'est-à-dire de la communication directe, immédiate, de la conscience avec l'être.

Dans l'ordre spéculatif, on a montré que, ni la logique, ni l'expérience externe, ni l'union de ces deux modes de connaissance ne suffisent à constituer les sciences : il y faut joindre, incessamment, ce contact spontané et intime avec la réalité, que l'on nomme intuition. Les mathématiques elles-mêmes, pour faire un choix entre tous les possibles que leur présente la pensée abstraite, font appel à un sens caché des harmonies réelles qui président aux lois de notre univers.

Dans l'ordre pratique, on a compris qu'il ne suffit pas à la volonté, pour faire le bien, d'en avoir la notion abstraite, mais qu'un accroissement et un ennoblissement de son énergie est nécessaire, et que cette vertu supérieure ne lui peut venir que d'une communion intime avec d'autres volontés, plus hautes et plus puissantes. "Dieu ne peut être la fin s'il n'est le principe," disait Pascal. Vouloir Dieu sans se donner à lui, afin que lui-même agisse en nous, c'est ne le vouloir que des lèvres.

On ne peut qu'applaudir, semble-t-il, à cette réhabilitation au sein de la vie humaine, du spontané, de l'intuitif, de l'instinct, de l'élan profond et libre de l'âme. Mais il y a lieu de se demander si, dans la direction de notre activité intellectuelle et morale, l'instinct et l'intuition doivent être substitués purement et simplement, à la science et à l'intelligence discursive, ou si la science conserve son originalité et sa valeur propre, en face des formes les plus hautes de l'instinct et de l'inspiration.

Or, s'il est vain de prétendre ramener l'instinct à la connaissance par concepts, et la religion à la science, il n'est pas moins contraire à la réalité de ne voir dans la science qu'une analyse artificielle et infidèle de la vie et de l'action créatrice. La science est l'effort de l'intelligence pour saisir, de la réalité, cet élément qu'on appelle l'ordre, la mesure, la loi, et dont l'existence n'est pas moins certaine et importante que la variété, la souplesse, la mobilité, la continuelle fraîcheur et nouveauté, par où se révèle l'action d'un pouvoir créateur.

La science est irréductible à la religion; ou plutôt toute religion est incomplète, étroite, artificielle, qui ne sait pas voir, dans le monde, l'œuvre vraiment divine, douée, par la toute-puissance et la toute-bonté, d'une existence propre et d'une ressemblance de la liberté divine. Dieu, disait Pascal, a voulu donner à ses créatures la dignité de la causalité. Et Platon:

"Dieu a créé le monde, parce qu'il est exempt d'envie. Il lui a donné la puissance d'imiter son divin modèle, et de se faire dieu lui-même, en quelque manière." Observer et admirer l'œuvre divine, ce n'est pas se détourner de Dieu.

Il serait donc téméraire de prétendre réserver la direction de nos pensées et de nos actes à l'intuition interne et à l'instinct, en prenant simplement le contre-pied de cet intellectualisme exclusif qui prétendait la réserver à la science positive et conceptuelle. Science et intuition, les choses et l'esprit, le milieu et la vie, la loi et la liberté, sont deux faces de l'être et du connaître, irréductibles l'une à l'autre.

S'ensuit-il que, pour remplir notre destinée, nous devions vivre deux vies totalement distinctes; que la religion se rapporte uniquement à notre vie intérieure, et que notre vie extérieure doive être abandonnée sans réserve à la science, à la force, à la brutale nécessité?

Le dualisme radical, ou séparation absolue de l'ordre matériel et de l'ordre moral, est, sans doute, une solution claire et commode du problème de la vie. Qu'importe, à l'âme qui s'est installée en Dieu, la conduite que tient, sur la terre, le corps auquel elle est juxtaposée? Mais cette solution sera jugée artificielle par les consciences qui s'interrogeront, sans parti pris théologique ou métaphysique, sur leur devoir et sur leur pouvoir.

L'homme doit réaliser toute la perfection dont il est capable, il doit, autant qu'il est en lui, imiter Dieu. Or il ne convient pas de se demander si Dieu est, exclusivement, parole, ou pensée, ou force, ou action: Dieu est l'harmonie, l'unité vivante de l'essence et de l'existence, c'est-à-dire de l'idéal et de la réalisation, de la vérité et de l'être.

L'homme qui se propose d'imiter Dieu doit faire un tout harmonieux de son être intérieur et de son existence externe, de son instinct et de son expérience, de ses inspirations et de ses déductions logiques, de son élan spontané et de sa dépendance à l'égard des choses.

Est-ce possible?

L'opinion suivant laquelle il faudrait opter entre l'instinct et la science, entre la spontanéité et l'intelligence, a sa source dans une théorie qui réduit l'intelligence à un mécanisme métaphysique, où des concepts abstraits se combinent entre eux suivant des lois de nécessité, comme se combinent les forces dans le monde physique. L'absolue inertie qui, dans cette théorie, est attribuée à l'intelligence, est évidemment incompatible avec l'absolue spontanéité que, réciproquement, on accorde à l'instinct. Et, dès lors, adopter l'un des deux termes, c'est rejeter l'autre.

Mais l'intelligence, ainsi conçue, est-elle bien toute l'intelligence? Il est remarquable que, si Kant et les métaphysiciens allemands se sont appliqués à dresser la table immuable de ce qu'ils appellent les catégories de l'entendement, les Descartes, les Platon s'abstinrent d'une telle recherche. Même les catégories d'Aristote, déterminées empiriquement, sont tout autre chose que les concepts *a priori* construits, suivant une formule, par les spéculatifs allemands. Au-dessus de l'intelligence purement logique Platon, Aristote, Descartes admettent, sous le nom de νοῦς ou de raison, une puissance de juger qui n'est pas l'application mécanique d'une formule, mais une pensée vivante, parente de l'être et de la vérité: Ἡ γὰρ νοῦ ἐνέργεια, ζωή, et, en ce qui concerne le νοῦς divin, ζωὴ ἀρίστη καὶ ἀΐδιος. Selon Descartes la raison, ou puissance de discerner, en toute matière, le vrai du faux, n'est pas la faculté d'appliquer une formule, mais le commerce intime et vivant de l'intelligence humaine avec l'être et avec la vérité. Cette raison a d'ailleurs besoin de culture: elle se forme par la réflexion sur les sciences et sur la vie.

Si, dans l'ordre intellectuel, il convient de distinguer entre entendement logique et raison vivante, il y a lieu, pareillement, dans l'ordre pratique, de distinguer entre instinct et liberté. Le terme d'instinct, en lui-même, évoque une idée de spontanéité. Le pur instinct comme premier principe, ce serait la spontanéité absolue, se suffisant, et suffisant à tout expliquer. Mais d'une telle force, qui se confondrait avec le hasard ou le destin, les philosophes classiques ont, de tout temps, distingué la puissance dont les effets se signalent par leur bonté, leur harmonie, leur beauté. La plus haute puissance d'action, selon eux, ce n'est pas la pure spontanéité, c'est la liberté. Or la liberté est faite, et de spontanéité et d'intelligence; non, sans doute, de cette intelligence, encore mécanique, qui, indifférente à la valeur des idées, se borne à les enchaîner logiquement entre elles, mais de cette souple et vivante intelligence, qui a affaire, par-delà les symboles, aux êtres eux-mêmes, et qui veut comprendre et apprécier, en même temps que constater et classer.

Qu'est-ce à dire, sinon qu'une même puissance, celle qu'Aristote appelait la raison, ὁ νοῦς, domine, et l'instinct et l'entendement logique; et que, dans leur union avec cette puissance, l'instinct comme l'entendement trouvent leur achèvement et leur perfection?

S'il en est ainsi, les expressions les plus hautes, et de l'instinct et de l'entendement logique, à savoir la religion et la science, ne sont pas deux étrangères et deux ennemies, entre lesquelles il soit impossible d'établir un accord et une pénétration. La raison est chez elle dans le domaine de la religion comme dans celui de la science; car la religion vraie est raisonnable, non moins que la science des réalités. La religion, comme disait Malebranche, est la raison s'unissant au cœur pour aller vers Dieu, comme la science est la raison guidant les sens et les rendant aptes à connaître les lois véritables de la nature.

Donc, ne craignons pas d'affirmer que l'objet essentiel de l'éducation, particulièrement à notre époque, est la réconciliation de la science, qui nous fait connaître l'action du milieu ou des choses sur la conscience humaine, et de la religion, qui donne à nos dispositions intérieures leur forme la plus haute et la plus belle. A cette réconciliation l'instinct et la science sont, par eux-mêmes, susceptibles de contribuer grandement. Mais cette œuvre est l'office propre et suprême de la raison, aux yeux de qui tout ce qui est, comme disait Aristote, a son principe dans l'unité intime du souverain intelligible et du souverain désirable.

C'est dans ce sens qu'est conçu le présent livre de M. St. G. L. Fox Pitt. Cette orientation nous paraît la bonne. Dans une telle doctrine se réunissent, d'accord avec les plus solides traditions de l'esprit humain, les deux tendances principales de la pensée contemporaine.

Agréez, je vous prie, cher Monsieur, l'assurance de ma haute considération et de mes sentiments bien cordialement dévoués.

ÉMILE BOUTROUX.

PARIS.
8 *janvier* 1916.

TRANSLATION OF LETTRE-PRÉFACE

By *Professor H. Wildon-Carr, D.Litt.*

DEAR SIR,

Forgive me if, in the present crisis, I find myself without the freedom of mind and the leisure needful for reflecting, as deeply as I could wish, on the important teaching in your book, to which one might apply the saying of Aristotle: καὶ τῷ ὄγκῳ μικρόν, δυνάμει καὶ τιμιότητι ὑπερέχει: "Small in volume, great in importance and value."

There is one point in particular that I should have liked to examine profoundly, following the lead your book gives us so clearly, and, to my thinking, so judiciously.

The man who faces the question how he ought to direct his life, in order to fulfil his end as man, sees before him two opposite paths, each of which presents itself as the true and only way: the one is from within outwards, from the man to things, from mind to nature: the other is from nature to mind, from environment to the consciousness, from things to the man. Two alternatives, said Horace, are offered me: *mihi res, aut me rebus subjungere.*

This everlasting alternative became in the last century the conflict of religion and science as guides of human life. According to the advocates of science, wisdom consists in the adaptation pure and simple of inner to outer, that is to say, of man to his environment, such as strictly objective observation makes it known to him. According to the advocates of religion, the mind eludes the clasp of science and finds, in its attachment to the Creator, the whole of the conditions of its own life.

It is undeniable that in the latter half of last century the methods and processes of the scientific way had become more

b 2

and more triumphant. Science invaded one by one every domain
from which it had seemed to be for ever excluded: life, the
soul, society, art, morals and even religion. Now if all that is
or can be, without exception, belong in very fact to science
and be consequently literally subject to scientific determinism,
what other object can human culture set before itself than that
of forming man for the kind of life which, according to the data
of science, the environment in which he is placed by nature
assigns him?

To many minds the victory of the scientific view seemed
absolute. Religion and morals, to their thinking, were reality
only in so far as they were branches of natural history.

But, for some time now, this purely objective conception of
things has been strongly disputed. We have come to see the
importance of the part which instinct plays, and how irreducible
it is to that abstract and reasoned knowledge of which positive
science is the most complete form. We have come to perceive
that instinct not only guides our physical life in the manner
most useful to it, but it furnishes the highest suggestions and
most generous impulses in the domain of the moral and religious
life itself.

Must not instinct, then, be a kind of direct and living perception of being, whilst science operates not on being itself, but
on the artificial symbols of it appropriate to our imagination and
to our understanding?

It is, speaking generally, a feature of recent speculations that
they have, in every domain, restored the value of instinct and
intuition, that is to say, of the direct immediate communication
of consciousness with being.

In the speculative order it has been shown that neither logic
nor external experience, nor the union of these two modes of
knowledge, are sufficient of themselves to constitute the sciences:
we must join with them unceasingly that spontaneous and intimate contact with reality, which we call intuition. Even mathe-

matics, in order to make its choice among all the possibles which abstract thought presents to it, makes appeal to a hidden sense of the real harmonies which preside over the laws of our universe.

In the practical order, we have come to understand that for right action it is not enough that the will should have the abstract notion of the good, there must also be a growth and heightening of its energy, and this superior strength can only come from an intimate communion with other wills, higher and stronger than itself. "God can only be the end if He be the original principle," said Pascal. To want God without giving ourself up to Him, in order that He Himself act in us, is to want Him with our lips only.

We cannot but be glad, it seems, at this rehabilitation within the bosom of human life, of the spontaneous, of the intuitive, of instinct, of the deep and free impulse of the soul. But we have to ask ourselves whether, in the direction of our intellectual and moral activity, instinct and intuition must be substituted purely and simply for science and discursive thought, or whether science can preserve its own originality and value, confronted with the higher forms of instinct and of inspiration.

Now if it be vain to attempt to bring instinct under knowledge by concepts, and religion under science, it is no less contrary to reality to see in science only an artificial and unfaithful analysis of life and of creative action. Science is the effort of the intellect to seize in the reality the element we call order, measure, law, the existence of which is no less certain and important than the variety, suppleness, mobility, continual freshness and novelty, by which the action of a creative power is revealed.

Science is incommensurable with religion; or rather, all religion is incomplete, narrow and artificial, which is unable to regard the world as a truly divine work endowed by supreme power and goodness with an existence of its own, and with a resemblance to the divine liberty. "God," said Pascal, "has willed to give to

His creatures the dignity of causality." And Plato: "God has created the world because He is free from envy. He has given it the power of imitating its divine model, and, in a manner, of making itself God." To regard the divine work, and wonder at it, is not to turn away from God.

It would be rash therefore to claim for inner intuition and instinct the exclusive direction of our thoughts and of our acts, simply taking intuition as the counterpart of that exclusive intellectualism which claims to reserve to itself positive and conceptual science. Science and intuition, things and mind, environment and life, law and liberty, are two aspects of being and knowing, irreducible one to the other.

Does it follow that to fulfil our end we must live two totally distinct lives; that religion is only concerned with our inner life while our external life must be unreservedly given over to science, to force, to brute necessity?

Radical dualism, or absolute separation of the material order from the moral order, is, no doubt, a clear and logically convenient solution of the problem of life. What matters, to the soul installed in God, the earthly conduct of the body to which it is conjoined? But such a solution will be judged artificial by the consciousness of all who without theological or metaphysical prejudice reflect on their duty and on their power.

Man must realise all the perfection of which he is capable; he must, as far as it is in him, imitate God. There is no need then that he ask himself whether God is, exclusively, word, or thought, or force, or action: God is the harmony, the living unity of essence and existence, that is to say, of the ideal and the real, of truth and being.

Whoever sets before himself the imitation of God must make of his inner being and his outer existence, of his instinct and his experience, of his inspirations and his logical deductions, of his spontaneous impulse and his dependence on things, one harmonious whole.

Is it possible?

The opinion according to which he must make a choice
between instinct and science, between spontaneity and intelligence, has its source in a theory which reduces intelligence to
a metaphysical mechanism which combines abstract concepts
together according to necessary laws, just as the forces in the
physical world are combined. The absolute inertia, which in
this theory we attribute to the intellect, is clearly incompatible
with the absolute spontaneity, which, reciprocally, we assign to
instinct. And, hence, to adopt one of the two terms is to reject
the other.

But is the intellect, so conceived, in very deed the whole
intellect? It is remarkable that while Kant and the German
metaphysicians occupied themselves in drawing up the fixed
table of what they call the categories of the understanding, such
a task is one on which the Descartes and Platos would not have
entered. Even the empirically determined categories of Aristotle
are of a different order from that of the concepts constructed
a priori, according to a formula, by the speculative Germans.
Above the purely logical intellect, Plato, Aristotle and Descartes
admit, under the name of νοῦς or reason, a power of judging
which is not the mechanical application of a formula, but a
living thought, begetter of being and truth: Ἡ γὰρ νοῦ ἐνέργεια
ζωή; and, in so far as it concerns the divine νοῦς, ζωὴ ἀρίστη καὶ
ἀΐδιος. According to Descartes, reason, or the power of dis-
cerning in all matter the true from the false, is not the faculty
of applying a formula, but the inward and living intercourse
of the human intellect with being and with truth. It is a reason
moreover in need of cultivation; it is formed by reflection on
the sciences and on life.

If, in the intellectual order, it is convenient to distinguish
between logical understanding and living reason, so likewise,
in the practical order, there is ground for distinguishing between
instinct and liberty. The term "instinct" in itself evokes an

idea of spontaneity. The pure instinct, as a first principle, would be absolute spontaneity, self-sufficing, and sufficing to explain everything. But from such a force, which would be one with chance or fate, the classical philosophers have always distinguished the power whose effects are characterised by goodness, harmony and beauty. The highest power of action, according to them, is not pure spontaneity; it is liberty. Now liberty is made of both spontaneity and intellect; not, doubtless, of that intellect which, still mechanical, is indifferent to the value of ideas, and limited to linking them logically together, but of that supple and living intellect which deals, through symbols, with beings themselves, and which would understand and appreciate whilst it describes and classifies.

Is not this in effect to say that one and the same power, the power which Aristotle called reason, νοῦς, over-rules both instinct and logical understanding, and that, in the union of these with reason, instinct as well as understanding find their achievement and their perfection?

If it be so, the highest expressions of instinct and of logical understanding, to wit, religion and science, are not strangers and enemies, between whom it is impossible to establish agreement and penetration. Reason is at home in the domain of religion as it is in that of science, because true religion is reasonable no less than the science of realities. Religion, as Malebranche said, is reason uniting itself to the heart that it may go toward God, as science is reason guiding the senses and making them fit to know the true laws of nature.

Let us not fear then to affirm that the essential object of education, particularly at this present time, is the reconciliation of science, which makes us know the action of the environment or of things on the human consciousness, with religion which gives to our inner dispositions their highest and most beautiful form. Instinct and science are capable of themselves of contributing greatly to this reconciliation. But this work is the supreme and especial function of reason, in whose regard whatever is, as Aristotle has said, has its principle in the intimate unity of what is supreme both as intelligible and as desirable.

It is with this aim that the present book of Mr St G. Lane Fox Pitt is conceived. The direction in which it points appears to me the right one. In such a doctrine are reunited, in accordance with the soundest traditions of the human mind, the two principal tendencies of contemporary thought.

Accept, dear Sir, I pray, the expression of my great regard and hearty good will.

ÉMILE BOUTROUX.

PREFACE TO FIRST EDITION

EXPERIMENTAL psychology has made considerable progress in recent years. Fresh knowledge as to the facts relating to the working of the human mind has been discovered; and a new terminology has been evolved.

It is the object of the present work to apply this knowledge to the elucidation of educational problems, in the hope that some of the confusions and difficulties which prevail, both in the public mind and in that of experts, may, to some extent at any rate, be cleared up. Much of the ground traversed will naturally be familiar to teachers and students of the subject; but the explanation offered of the psychical processes involved in the art of pedagogy may be helpful in the endeavour of reformers to improve and systematise the somewhat chaotic methods at present in vogue.

The chief difficulty encountered, in all attempts at the effective presentment of unfamiliar ideas, consists in the detection and adaptation of a suitable terminology. To some extent, no doubt, this difficulty can be met by the practice of paraphrasing, but the employment of a precise and systematic nomenclature is also important. It is not improbable that many readers may be irritated and even alienated by the frequent use in these pages of the word "complex" for the purpose of indicating those egocentric phases of mind, which are more usually, if more vaguely, denominated by the words memory, mood, or motive. The term "complex" is now, however, current and accepted in all the more important works, recently issued, which bear upon medical, or abnormal psychology and kindred subjects. The study of abnormal psychology has helped to reveal the *rationale* and *modus operandi* of thought and feeling, and the term "complex" has been used to designate an undoubted discovery, arising out of this study, as to the mode in which specific psycho-physical processes occur and function, not only in morbid conditions of mind and body, but also in normal life. The author hopes, therefore, that its use may be admitted here as being neither arbitrary, nor pedantic.

Great stress has been laid on the educational value of high ideals: upon their inculcation and growth. With this end in view an attempt is made to indicate certain important distinctions and discriminations, which are essential preliminaries to that true unification of thought lying at the root of universal beliefs. It is easy enough to profess admiration for the ideal human qualities: charity, tolerance, impartiality, honesty and the like; but it is very difficult to understand why, in practice, these ideals should so often be disregarded, not to say systematically ignored. The use of conventional terms is often supposed to supply an explanation. "Mystery," "sin," "selfishness," "disobedience," "malice," "ignorance" are all made to serve their turn. Words, however, are not explanations. Explanations are the product of experience and meditation through which there is an awakening of the higher faculties of insight and understanding.

It is, of course, generally recognised that certain familiar expressions convey varying implications according to the context in which they occur; and that this represents a common linguistic difficulty. The inconvenience of this ambiguity, however, becomes a serious trouble when, as sometimes happens, the different meanings attached to the same word are diametrically opposed. Thus "charity" suggests both "self-denial" and "self-gratification" in varying degrees dependent on our preconceptions as to the theory of "self." So it is with "tolerance," "impartiality" and "honesty."

In the contemplation of the huge extent of human suffering some are apt to grow impatient and to demand the discovery of an immediate and final remedy. In this search the trend of thought seems to oscillate between one extreme and another. At one time the prevailing view is directed towards making exaggerated claims for the importance of the inner life, and at other times it is directed towards an exaggeration of the importance of "environment." It is one of the main objects of these pages to indicate the middle path, which avoids these two extremes.

St G. L. F. P.

Travellers' Club,
Pall Mall, London.
19 *October* 1913.

TABLE OF CONTENTS

CHAPTER I

HUMAN PERSONALITY

IT is a commonplace saying that ignorance and prejudice die hard. It is not, however, so easily perceived that the death of this ignorance and prejudice almost invariably gives rise to their re-birth in new forms which may be no nearer to the expression of the truth than the old forms they have replaced. So also is there re-birth of universal truths, of those grand synthetic generalizations, which obtain with more or less persistence among all peoples and in all times. With truth there can be nothing fundamentally new, yet its re-expression in terms of current experience may come with all the force and attractiveness of novelty. But the barrier to its reception is just this ignorance and prejudice in the public mind, which it is the function of education to remove. Thus we find many words and phrases in the literature of all nations bearing testimony to the confused and contradictory nature of current beliefs and to the survival of old notions as to the meaning and import of the human personality. These beliefs fall into two main classes. According to the first and more popular class, a "person" is the combination of a body, or physical organism, with a permanent, more or less independent, soul-entity which animates it; and for this class the great work of education consists in the harmonising of these two factors. With the second class of beliefs, the body is regarded as the ultimate fact; the mind or character being considered as a quality or function of the physical organism, to be developed like a plant by contact with a suitable "environment." The propounders of this doctrine, although admitting that much may be due to "heredity," insist, nevertheless, that the child is born fundamentally "good," and that the whole function of education is the skilful drawing out of its innate excellences.

Now controversialists holding opposed doctrines, while vainly imagining that they have established the validity of their own thesis by an elaborate refutation of their opponents' point of view, are apt to exclaim "Both doctrines cannot be true." Well, perhaps not, but they can both be false, as indeed, almost invariably, they are.

Common ground as between opponents, there necessarily must be. There is common ground in language, though it nearly always presents difficulties. Obviously too, opponents share much in their familiar environments. In expressing differences of opinion, whether in discussion or in exposition, it is no doubt well to discover as much common ground as is strictly relevant, even to insist upon it; but where we find points of fundamental difference it is cowardly and dishonest to ignore them, or to slur them over. The frank acknowledgment of serious differences often helps towards their removal and paves the way towards mutual understanding. Our object, certainly, should be to avoid barren controversies, especially such as are mainly verbal. In previous editions the term "psychology" often occurred. This word has now become so ambiguous owing to its peculiar use in different schools of thought that in the present edition its occurrence is much less frequent. There are for example "dualistic" psychologies and "monistic" psychologies. The presentation of life and thought sketched in these pages is neither monistic, nor is it dualistic. Our basis may, therefore, be conveniently indicated by the compound word "psychophysical" to escape from this ambiguity. According to a dualistic system, living organisms are compounded arbitrarily out of two factors which are said to be absolutely distinct, though they interact. E. B. Tylor gave the name "animism" to this system. In the "animistic" view of life, "spirits" are separate entities capable of existing and disporting themselves wholly apart from, and quite independently of, any physical organism. According to a "monistic" or "materialistic" view, mind is a mere function of matter, while matter itself is regarded as the ultimate "reality." Inasmuch as this form of psychology is concerned primarily with the *behaviour* of the organism, it is often spoken of as "behaviourism."

Crude generalizations of either kind must as far as possible be avoided and their special nomenclature discarded, in order to clear the mind from misconception preparatory to giving serious and unbiased consideration to the results and conclusions of modern research on fundamental problems.

This done, it may be stated positively, as a fact which has been clearly demonstrated, that the human personality under a thoroughgoing analysis exhibits, not a permanent and unalterably separate entity, but a vast combination or aggregation of variegated, fluctuating, loosely organised and interdependent physical and psychic phases and potentialities, of which no more than a minute fragment makes its presence manifest to our ordinary, or "normal" waking consciousness. An illustration, offered by the late Mr Frederick Myers, will be found helpful provided that the analogy is not pressed too far. It compares personality to an iceberg, ever changing in structure and substance, the great bulk of which is always invisible and submerged. This iceberg simile is defective in that it might suggest a certain *rigidity of structure* as a quality of personality, as also a certain *fixity* in the proportion between its visible and invisible factors. The periodic emergence of a whale above the surface of the ocean might, in these respects, offer a more useful figure.

As we approach to anything in the nature of fixity and permanence so we approach the impersonal.

We are all familiar with such phrases as being or not being in a "mood" for anything: we speak of an attentive or a careless mood, a pleasant or a nasty mood, etc. We recognise the mental phenomena to which such phrases apply and as a rule we accept them as important factors in our lives, but we often misinterpret their meaning or put them down as inexplicable.

Scientific research explains the mystery by indicating the nature of the human personality. The evidences of recent research have shown that an individual is composed of a vast number and great variety of correlated psycho-physical complexes[1].

A "complex" may be defined as a group[2] or system or aggregate of associated or combined ideas[3], linked together in some experience, or succession of experiences, with corresponding emotions, perceptions, "memories," interests, range of beliefs, actions and volitions; linked in such a manner as to be capable of so dominating certain functions of the brain and nervous system as to generate a consciousness[4], or a feeling in conjunction

---

[1] The expression "psycho-physical complex," usually abbreviated throughout as *complex*, does not necessarily imply any specifically pathological condition as assumed in the writings of "psychoanalysts." The word "complex" is used here as the equivalent of the Latin *complexus*, i.e., a "complex whole" (see *Concise Oxford Dictionary*, under this head). It means simply a *factor* in the ordinary composition and growth of personality, as revealed by analysis, or critical examination of the processes of life and mind.

[2] Neither "group," nor "system," nor "aggregate" is quite a suitable term to express that arrangement of ideas associated or combined in a complex. "Vortex" might perhaps serve, though it would too much suggest analogy with fluid motion. "Dynamic or syndynamic system" would probably be the least objectionable.

[3] There may be philosophical objections to the treatment of ideas as entities or units, just as there may be metaphysical objections to the hypothetical atoms and molecules with which science has made us conceptually familiar. In both cases, however, it is mainly a question of practical convenience in nomenclature and symbolism. Further, with ideas it might even seem expedient to use an extended similitude, and speak of *associated* ideas as those grouped by a process of *admixture* or *solution*, while *concepts* might be held to represent those *combined* by a process of natural affinity.

[4] The term "consciousness" implies transitory phases of *mind*, yielding conditions of *awareness* in great variety. These conditions usually involve the focusing of attention upon specific phenomena. The term "subconscious," as applied to mind, indicates such conditions of its development as are differentially active, while not specifically focused, and are yet capable of being focused. "Unconscious mind" is used to denote the potentiality of

with those ideas, of egoistic or individualistic self-hood, however transitory and imperfect in its manifestation.

The stimulation of one element of a complex, generally speaking, excites activity in some or all of the rest. Notwithstanding their transitory independence in functioning, all complexes are really allied to one another, more or less correlated and interdependent, but are imperfectly co-ordinated in their manifestation. According to the rise and fall of different complexes in the field of vivid or focused consciousness, or in a less degree according to their tendency to assert themselves subconsciously, so is one's change of mood.

To speak, as many do, of *the* subconscious "mind" or "self" is very misleading. There is no definite self-entity that remains always subconscious, nor, for that matter, does there exist any veritable psychic mass, called by the Freudians "the unconscious," which they tell us is invariably fixed somewhere in the personality out of all contact with consciousness. The most trustworthy results of modern research confirm the belief of early investigators that all complexes, which, for the time being, are below the threshold of consciousness, however deeply they may be imbedded in oblivion, however they may be isolated by dissociation or by inversion, or however they may be clustered together in groups by their affinities, are ever tending by reason of their inherent vitality to assert themselves in the personality's functioning in any way that they can find power and opportunity to do so effectually. An individual may not be fully, or indeed at all aware of this tendency, or of its manner of functioning, but the tendency is a factor nevertheless.

mind, i.e., mind which is psychically undeveloped, individually un-differentiated, or unprepared for focusing, as being *outside* human consciousness in the sense of never having been assimilated with it. It should be noted in this connection that Dr Sigmund Freud, of Vienna, and his school speak of "*the unconscious*" as covering all those mental phases which, in accordance with the above nomenclature, should be called *dissociated subconscious* activities.

The element of "emotion," sometimes called "feeling," is of great importance in the functioning of a complex, as determining its relative capacity for persistent and isolated activity, and is dealt with more fully in a separate chapter. It will suffice for the moment to say that the term "emotion" is used here as an expression for the energy of likes and dislikes, as also for such comparative notions as "preferences" and "choice of evils," which are characteristic of the bulk of our ordinary thoughts. As Sir Charles Sherrington aptly remarks in his *Integrative Action of the Nervous System*: "Emotion 'moves' us, hence the word itself." We should bear in mind, however, to avoid confusion, that the more familiar signification attached to the term is usually expressive of some manifestation of emotional excess or discord.

The formulation of psycho-physical complexes was foreshadowed, though somewhat vaguely, by Herbart in his enunciation of what he terms "apperception masses."

The types of complexes are very various; they may be classified roughly as belonging to three main orders:

1. The minor variety, which is by far the most numerous kind, and is, generally speaking, the more limited in its range and more transitory. These complexes have their genesis in what are ordinarily called "events," or specific experiences; as for example a particular meal, a game, a privation, a lesson, an accident, a dispute, a punishment, an illness, a success or a failure. Even such a conglomerate of events, closely associated in our thoughts as constituting in themselves the peculiar incidents of our lives in the nature of "personal experiences" great or small, forms the basis of a minor complex.

2. The intermediate variety, comprising various intellectual and moral concepts of a co-ordinating, syndynamic and synthetic nature. These complexes have definite relations to certain specific "environments," both material and psychic. To this order, viewed as transcending mere personal experiences, belong our systematised notions of (*a*) the physical and biological worlds,

for example, heat and cold, light, colour, electricity, sound, weight, gravitational attraction, number, time, space, force, motion, energy, radiation, and the qualities and composition of matter; thus also our ideas of life, action and reflex, decay, disease and death, the bodily organs and senses, hunger, nourishment, and growth; (b) moral qualities, such as kindness and cruelty, diligence and idleness, intelligence and stupidity, honesty and deceit, generosity and greed, modesty and boastfulness, individual responsibility and reciprocal obligations; (c) institutional ideas, customs, ordinances, social order and distinctions, history, geography, laws of justice, equity, and speech. The element of personal experience, although an undoubted factor in the development and acquisition of all such concepts, is subordinated to the idea of their universality. These complexes are in fact the equivalents of "concepts" in the philosophic or scientific sense.

3. The Great Complex[1], i.e., the personality or character as a co-ordinated whole. This complex, though rarely awakened as a vivid synthetic consciousness, shows a tendency towards an occasional and imperfect emergence as "conscience." It is in complete harmony within, and with the Universal Life, when truly awakened; and it gains, thereby, infinite mental freedom and power.

The strength and worth of our *personality* are determined by the quality, the mobility, the elasticity and the co-ordination of the complexes out of which it is composed.

At any moment a specific complex, or several simultaneously (forming a "co-consciousness"), may emerge into the field of normal, waking, focused or vivid consciousness. The rest, the vast majority, remain for the time being submerged; exercising, no doubt, a vague kind of subtle influence in our thoughts and

---

[1] The phrase "Great Complex" is borrowed from the *Mahā-Sudassana-Sutanta*; translated by Prof. Rhys Davids in the *Sacred Books of the Buddhists*. See Vol. III, p. 214 *note*.

actions, though "automatically," unvolitionally and, so to speak, surreptitiously. There is an abundance of evidence, however, that while submerged in subconscious strata of our existence, our dormant complexes do not persist in a static condition, but are subject to continual change. Nor do they remain isolated, for it has been demonstrated by means of hypnotic experiments[1] that, after successive emergence, they reappear modified by the assimilation of qualities and tendencies derived from allied or complementary complexes; even, be it said (though the fact is generally disputed), by psychic interaction with the subconscious elements of other personalities[2].

The same ideas, or, to speak more correctly, similar concepts, may occur in various complexes, though allied to different feelings. Thus, for example, the idea *food* would present itself as attractive or the reverse according to the condition of the stomach and nervous system, functioning with the mood then dominant.

Let us now consider the origin and growth of complexes. They are the outcome of experience, both physical and psychical, though to what degree or in what manner respectively we shall not attempt to consider here. It will be enough at this juncture to point out that, although the distinction made between the physical instrument of thought and the psychical powers is not to be regarded as amounting to independence, or absolute separateness of function, yet for the better understanding of educational processes precise terminological definitions of these fundamental concepts are of very great scientific importance. The clearly

[1] See *The Dissociation of a Personality* by Morton Prince, M.D. (Longmans & Co.). Dr Prince shows that complexes, even when highly dissociated, can merge themselves into one another while they are below the threshold of consciousness.

[2] Professor Henri Bergson, de l'Académie française, in a lecture delivered in London, said he considered the evidence in support of the belief in subconscious interaction of thought and feeling between different individuals, was positively overwhelming. He insisted that this kind of "psychic osmosis" was always in action, more or less, though generally unnoticed; but suggested that a too erratic or pronounced development of the process would become "highly embarrassing."

established scientific data and formulae of the physical world, relating as they do to phenomena so remote from the processes usually called psychical, may of course be treated, for specific practical purposes, as pertaining to forces operating independently of ordinary thought. There is, however, a danger in doing this arbitrarily or dogmatically. The danger arises out of a forgetfulness of the innumerable changes which such data and formulae have undergone in the past and are continually undergoing: a forgetfulness which is liable to engender a too arrogant belief in their absolutely fixed and universal nature; and in the infallibility, for all purposes, of the "scientific method." This is not meant by way of detracting from the value of the scientific method as an instrument of research; nor is it intended as disparaging its important achievements in practical spheres. It is merely a reminder that the method is based upon the systematic observation and correlation of phenomena or *appearances*, which sometimes prove deceptive. To illustrate the danger incurred by too strong an insistence upon universality inhering in the findings of the scientific method, attention need only be drawn to the confusion and revolutionary effects brought recently into the scientific world through the advent of the principles of relativity.

It cannot be too strongly insisted upon that complexes are not static entities, but that they are each one ever changing and developing through their tendency to strengthen and perpetuate themselves by adaptation to or assimilation with their respective environments or that aspect of real life to which they are complementary in the existing world "outside." In this struggle our various complexes compete, conflict and co-operate. In other words, each complex "ego" seeking intermittently to assimilate or to destroy the "non-ego" gives rise to a change in both. It is this process which is most important and obtrusive in the functioning of individualised life.

Vision, in a spiritual sense, is one of a complex's manifold phases, dependent on the manner of its emergence into vivid consciousness. A complex has many phases. The word may therefore be said to express, in a comprehensive fashion, the embodiment, potentiality, continuity, cause and outcome of *specific experience*. It is sometimes the equivalent of what we vaguely call a "habit." Its essential mark, however, is its power, latent or active, of generating a feeling and awareness of definite, though transitory, self-hood. It is just because all complex *subjects* can be postulated as *objects* of thought, that they can never be properly regarded as separate, unconditioned, or permanent. The "vision" generated through their strongly emotional emergence is sometimes liable to inversion (see Chapter VIII). It might perhaps be asked whether a word, with so elastic a signification, is really of much value; and indeed some exception has been taken to its use on the ground that it "covers almost all mental processes as well as almost all physical conditions." But is this objection fair? Would it not be as reasonable to object to the phrase "chemical compound," because it covers practically every variety of material object? The same chemical substance may occur as a solid, a liquid, a gas, as a crystalline or an amorphous material, as also in allotropic varieties. We must have a word to connote those recurrent, intermittent and persistent egocentric or individualistic phases, the functioning of which helps to explain and simplify the various processes made manifest in personality. Herbart's phrase "apperception masses" is certainly not more suitable. *Spirit, soul, will* and *mind* are all too ambiguous, and, although more familiar, they are all much discredited. *Mood* is too vague, so are *habit, memory* and *motive*. What serious objection is there to *complex*? It has already come into use, and it is readily adopted as soon as it ceases to sound unfamiliar.

Now each fresh stimulative contact of the organism with some chosen or "accidental"[1] environment makes an addition

[1] An environment is called "accidental" when its presence is unexpected, or unusual; or where there is an absence of full awareness as to its relativity and proximity to the occasion. (See Chapter VI.)

to, or some modification in, one or more of our complexes; so also when we "reflect," "reason," or "strive," the mental operation involved implies some interaction between the complexes; while the relatively exclusive absorption, or concentration of consciousness, in one complex, such as is characteristic of intense emotion, great interest, idle brooding, or preoccupation of the mind with a " fixed idea," may tend to the isolation of that complex and facilitate its persistence in a more or less "dissociated"[1] form. These relative dissociations determine the varying degrees of discontinuity and inconsistency in our modes of thought. Thus they represent, when strongly developed, those habit-bred and emotionally-barricaded dispositions which result in obstinacy, intolerance, fanaticism, meanness or similar personal incongruities. Assuming then that the advancement, or, as some would say, the awakening, of high character is the supreme aim of education, it must be obvious, from what has been said, that exclusive or too persistent concentration of consciousness in particular complexes is not advantageous, but the reverse. The right process for such an awakening is the harmonious development of various minor complexes in co-ordination with, and in subordination to, the intermediate complexes, in the first place, and then finally with the Great Complex, in so far as its awakening may be rendered possible. This later aspect of the problem is further considered in the chapter dealing with ideals.

The spontaneous tendency of complexes to assimilate one another may be greatly reinforced by conscious effort, in conjunction with suitable externals in the shape of apparatus

---

[1] Objection has been raised to this use of the word *dissociated* on the ground that it may be taken to imply the disruption of what was once united; but the term *dissociation* is often used in psychological writings as meaning merely *imperfectly assimilated,* or relatively isolated in functioning. It is generally in this sense that it is employed here. It should be remembered, however, that dissociations are either rudimentary or morbid conditions and that these should not be confused with our powers of co-ordinate abstraction, which involve voluntary mental detachments and the purposeful concentration of thought.

for illustration. In all individuals there are certain complexes which are, so to speak, near the surface, and thus more easily accessible. A skilled teacher will, therefore, by suggestion, endeavour to connect the subject he proposes to introduce to his pupils with some familiar group of ideas and interests. In this way the mind which is brought into action will be an associated system of complexes, already manufactured as it were, for the purpose of receiving instruction. And indeed it is generally admitted that the best form of "discipline" which can be employed is self-discipline; namely the concentrated attention of the pupil, stimulated by a genuine interest in the subject itself, or by devotion to noble ideals, rather than by fear of the consequences of inattention and neglect.

One of the most important facts, which the investigations of modern science have revealed, is the extremely limited range of choice, in the determination of his conduct, which falls to the lot of the average child, or indeed, for that matter, of the average human being. Each complex, or group of complexes, has its own sphere of freedom of action and volition. In the actual practical life of an individual he becomes aware, though without full comprehension of its meaning, of an occasional conflict of his numerous spheres of thought and action.

For the great majority of mankind, it is not possible that they should be given what they want; nor is it possible that forthwith they should be able to get for themselves what they want, or what they believe to be for their good and that it is right they should have. Their beliefs and wishes are closely allied, indeed almost interchangeable, but they vary from time to time; and, in their fluctuations, they mingle and conflict. True liberty or true freedom, therefore, is not a mere condition of our outward life that can be arbitrarily "given" or "taken away" by economic systems, by social conventions, and by political institutions. True freedom is a quality which springs from within and has to be gained by effort and perseverance, for freedom means a release

from bonds mostly of our own forging—bonds, that is to say,
which arise from a conflict of our wants, needs and interests.
Until our wants are gratified, we are apt to ignore their effects,
or how these effects may conflict with other wants that we expect
to be able to gratify as they arise. It follows, therefore, that the
power, above all others, which can stimulate effort and make it
effective in the direction of gaining mental freedom, is the
assimilation of right ideas to the extent of generating true convictions, or what are termed correct points of view. Now specific
convictions engender, or are allied to, specific feelings; and a
conflict of feelings brings about that condition of mind which
we speak of as "a lack of liberty." Harmonious feelings, on the
contrary, bring a *sense of freedom*; that is to say, the wish or
craving to do something we cannot do, or have difficulty in
doing, or the desire to avoid having to do distasteful things, is
in abeyance. Therefore the test of right ideas and points of view
is their power to harmonise and resolve the scattered contents
of our manifold minor complexes in relation to one another and
to some of those complexes which belong to a higher order, so
engendering an enduring sense of freedom and power. The
awakening of such true convictions is the real meaning of *revelation*. We may pass our lives in the repeated contemplation of
various phenomena, the connection between which is not
suspected, when suddenly there arises a perception of their true
relationship. What is this but a revelation?

Living in a damp cold climate we notice that grass will not
grow well under a big tree. We also notice that on the north
side of a wall our gardens will not flourish. From these and
similar phenomena we infer that sunlight is needed for vegetation. Most of us feel brighter, more cheerful and in better
health with much sunlight. The idea grows on us that sunlight
is not only a good thing, but that the more we can get of it the
better. We congratulate one another on the brightness and
warmth of "fine" weather and deplore the coming of cold and

damp. But let us visit a very dry hot climate, and the condition
of things is reversed. We find that vegetation flourishes most
luxuriantly under the shade of a cliff, and everything exposed to
the open sunlight is dried up. People congratulate themselves
on the presence of clouds and rain. Comparisons suggest themselves to our minds; and, by degrees to some, to others suddenly,
there dawns upon our minds the ideas of moderation, proportion,
balance. If now our complexes are mobile, that is to say if they
are not charged too strongly with the tenacity of emotion, which
tends by dissociations to restrict and obstruct the reception of new
ideas, this sense of moderation once gained in certain connec-
tions will rapidly spread to others.

The laws which govern the emergence of complexes and the
manner of their emergence are roughly speaking fourfold. Each
complex has its own dynamic and inherent forces, which will,
after a certain lapse of time and change of physical condition,
bring it to the surface of its own accord, as for example in moods
and dreams. Then there is an emergence due to the exercise of
the senses. Next there is an emergence possible in response to
verbal suggestion. And finally there are the emergences due to
our meditations. One might add, of course, a composite cause
of emergence due to an indeterminate combination of any or
all of the above causes.

Given favourable conditions and opportunities for their emergence from subconsciousness, complexes, either singly or associated in groups, follow cyclic phases in their development: first
there is a struggle for their emergence in consciousness and
actions, then comes a temporary fulfilment or gratification,
followed by the relative exhaustion of their active energies and
finally their relapse again into subconsciousness. The effects of
music may well be referred to in this connection. By *association*
or *affinity* a simple melody, harmonising with the emotional
element of some complex, stimulates its emergence into consciousness and tends to give it a generally pleasurable interpreta-

tion; while a composition of wider scope will evoke several
similar or contrasted complexes, skilfully juxtaposed, in such a
manner that they become blended by a sequence or current
of feeling into a relevant mood. Thus music of the highest
order may be defined as compositions proved by experience to
be most efficacious in these unifying qualities. This blending
process is similarly the characteristic mark of true wit, genuine
humour, the higher drama, poetry, and the fine arts generally.

Space would not allow of a very full discussion of the experimental investigations which have led up to the generalizations
and conclusions arrived at. But it may be stated that the author
has himself made innumerable experiments on his own personality
extending over a great number of years. With the help of
anaesthetics and other expedients, he has done much to verify,
correct and explore the work of other investigators. The serious
student, however, may be referred to the various medical and
scientific journals and the proceedings of numerous learned
societies. The following books may also be specially recommended: *The Integrative Action of the Nervous System*, by Sir
Charles Sherrington, P.R.S., *Bodily Changes in Pain, Fear,
Hunger and Rage*, by Professor Cannon, of Harvard University,
Problems of Dynamic Psychology, by Dr John T. MacCurdy
(Cambridge University Press), *The Major Symptoms of Hysteria*,
by Professor Pierre Janet (Macmillan) and the author's own book
—*Free Will and Destiny* (Constable).

The following extract from Professor Janet's book, just cited,
well illustrates what has been called a "dissociated" complex of
an extreme type. The case will be found on page 29 *et seq.*
of the second edition of that work:

A fourth and last observation, for I insist upon relating to you a great
number of instructive examples. We come back to the common story
of a young girl of twenty years old, called Irène, whom despair, caused
by her mother's death, has made ill. We must remember that this
woman's death had been very moving and dramatic....

The poor woman, who had reached the last stage of consumption, lived alone with her daughter in a poor garret. Death came slowly with suffocation, blood vomiting, and all its frightful procession of symptoms. The girl struggled hopelessly against the impossible. She watched her mother during sixty nights, working at her sewing-machine to earn a few pennies necessary to sustain their lives. After the mother's death she tried to revive the corpse, to call the breath back again; then, as she put the limbs upright, the body fell to the floor, and it took infinite exertion to lift it up again into the bed.

You may picture to yourself all that frightful scene. Some time after the funeral curious and impressive symptoms began. It was one of the most splendid cases of somnambulism (i.e., the functioning of a dissociated complex) I ever saw.

The crises lasted for hours, and they show a splendid dramatic performance, for no actress could rehearse those lugubrious scenes with such perfection. The young girl has the singular habit of acting again all the events that took place at her mother's death, without forgetting the least detail. Sometimes she only speaks, relating all that happened with great volubility, putting questions and answers in turn, or asking questions only, and seeming to listen for the answer; sometimes she only sees the sight, looking with frightened face and staring on the various scenes, and acting according to what she sees. At other times, she combines all hallucinations, words, and acts, and seems to play a very singular drama. When, in her dream, death has taken place, she carries on the same idea, and makes everything ready for her own suicide. She discusses it aloud, seems to speak with her mother, to receive advice from her; she fancies she will try to be run over by a locomotive. That detail is also a recollection of a real event of her life. She fancies she is on the way, and stretches herself out on the floor of the room, waiting for death with mingled dread and impatience. She poses, and wears on her face expressions really worthy of admiration, which remain fixed during several minutes. The train arrives before her staring eyes, she utters a terrible shriek, and falls back motionless as if she were dead. She soon gets up and begins acting over again one of the preceding scenes. In fact one of the characteristics of these somnambulisms is that they repeat themselves indefinitely. Not only the different attacks are always exactly alike, repeating the same movements, expressions, and words, but in the course of the same attack, when it has lasted a certain time, the same scene may be repeated again exactly in the same way five or ten times. At last the agitation seems to wear out, the dream grows less clear, and, gradually or suddenly, according to the cases, the patient comes back to her normal consciousness, takes up her ordinary business, quite undisturbed by what has happened.

Janet deals with several similar cases, and shows that the dissociations are governed by laws which have been known for a long time, but he looks upon Irène's case as typical. On page 37 he says:

Let us take up the case of that young girl, Irène, who acts during her somnambulism the scene of her mother's death with such apparent precision. Let us watch her during the intervals of her fits, during the period in which she seems to be normal; we shall soon notice that even at that time she is different from what she was before. Her relatives, when she was conveyed to the hospital, said to us: "She has grown callous and insensible, she has soon forgotten her mother's death and she does not seem to remember her illness." That remark seems amazing; it is, however, true that this young girl is unable to tell us what brought about her illness, for the good reason that she has quite forgotten the dramatic event that happened three months ago. "I know very well that my mother is dead," she says, "since I have been told so several times, since I see her no more, and since I am in mourning; but I really feel astonished at it. When did she die? What did she die from? Was I not by her to take care of her? There is something I do not understand. Why, loving her as I did, do I not feel more sorrow for her death? I can't grieve; I feel as if her absence were nothing to me, as if she were travelling and would soon be back." The same thing happens if you put to her questions about any of the events that occurred during those three months before her mother's death. If you ask her about the illness, the mishaps, the nightly staying up, anxieties about money, the quarrels with her drunken father—all these things have quite vanished from her mind. If we had time to dwell upon that case, we should have seen there many curious instances: the filial love, the feeling of affection she had felt for her mother, have quite vanished. It looks as if there was a gap as well in the feelings as in the memory. But I shall insist only on one point: the loss of memory bears not only, as is generally believed, on the period of somnambulism, on the scene of delirium; but the loss of memory bears also on the event that has given birth to that delirium, on all the facts that are connected with it, and on the feelings that are connected with it. This very important remark may be extended to all the other cases I have related.

This evidence of the close connection between the emotional character of a complex, and its capacity for carrying the "memory" of an experience with that character, is of great interest and value. Irène's case shows how such intense emotions, developing hallucinations as they do, may so dissociate a complex as to throw the whole order and arrangement of our lives out of gear. Inasmuch, however, as the emotional element supplies, or rather concentrates, the driving power of our activities in the early stages of our mental growth, it is of great importance that we should make a special effort to understand its true meaning and function.

Such extreme manifestations of emotional disorder, as in Janet's case just cited, are fortunately of very rare occurrence, but few of us are altogether exempt from milder forms of the same species of disturbance. As Janet says on page 23 of the same work:

Somnambulism has too long been considered as a rare phenomenon, impossible to explain, that adds itself to the habitual troubles of neuropaths. To me somnambulism is, on the contrary, extremely frequent under various forms that more or less conceal it. Somnambulism does not add itself to all sorts of neuropathic troubles; it constitutes the material point of a peculiar neurosis—hysteria. If one understands somnambulism well, one is, I believe, capable of understanding all hysterical phases that are more or less constructed on the same model.

We are all familiar with "fits of temper"; with our numerous anxieties and worries about trifles, or as we say colloquially "about nothing." We hear of nervous break-downs, consequent upon overwork or strain, which can be ameliorated or cured by change of scene. These and similar ailments, at times attributed to the hurry and stress of modern civilised life, at others to "heredity" or some other convenient expression to cover our ignorance, are, in fact, no more than manifestations of dissociative derangements of the healthy and harmonious current of our individual lives. All these troubles, except in rarer cases where they arise from veritable organic lesions, represent specific emergences of complexes, partly isolated by emotional excess. When Janet speaks of "somnambulisms" he implies the emergence of dissociated complexes, but it should be mentioned, in order to avoid any misunderstanding, that the phrase "psycho-physical complex" as defined and classified in the early part of this chapter is not in general use so far. Janet, instead of using the term "complex" in this connection, speaks of specific "psychological systems," which comes much to the same thing. It is generally supposed that somnambulisms are due to certain "affecting events," which is no doubt true as to the form they assume, but it should not be forgotten that if there were no dissociated (or partly dissociated) complexes latent, the "affecting events" themselves would not have occurred. This is fairly well indicated by Janet in his review of a large number of cases.

What, then, is emotion? It is none other than our vital energy, which is not, as commonly supposed, a quality evenly distributed throughout the organism. The evidence is over-whelming, not only in pathological conditions, but in normal life, that vital energy manifests itself in the nervous, visceral and vascular systems with such startling alternations as accord with definite psychological changes. That power, above all others, which determines the distribution of vital energy, whether latent or active, is undoubtedly our conscious life; but it is also clearly demonstrable that, irrespective of any definite conscious acts, our various complexes can and do accumulate a store of potential energy by a process of unconscious absorption from allied or complementary complexes. The energy thus transferred and absorbed is, in a sense, *transformed*, becoming particularised and fixed for service in the acquiring complexes. This process must be considered morbid or healthy according to the degree in which harmonious conditions are thereby impaired or pre-served in the whole organism. *Dissociation* in complexes (or a clustered group of complexes) may thus be characterised by their selfish greed of gain in the acquisition or retention of power. Thus also dissociated complexes become elements of discord in our higher individual growth. Obviously, however, no individual in the ordinary course of life can be entirely exempted from some sort of discord, though he may be relatively free from pronounced dissociations, but incipient dissociation there always is; and it is apt to grow by what may be called a parasitic process. A complex having in this manner grasped sufficient power from other complexes so as to enfeeble them, the growing dissociation may succeed in so dominating a personality as to develop a normally egoistic phase, or, more commonly, so as to express itself chaotically, in violent and explosive discharges of its energy, as for example in fits of rage.

It is true, no doubt, that some of the organism's vital energy is generally distributed, and not specifically allocated in complexes, so that it is partly free and partly fixed, and that some of this fixation may be comparatively harmless. In any case, dissociations are not all equally malignant, that is to say, equally harmful to our intellectual and moral growth, but they are always a source of danger. It is a very common though fallacious notion that some intense preoccupation with an absorbing object or idea is the only way to "get things done." Intense preoccupation of this kind may certainly be effective in getting something done, but it is of doubtful abiding worth, for the idea itself is apt, in the process, to become inverted, consequently what is "done" might better have been left undone.

It is not to be assumed from this, that all deep meditation is to be avoided. On the contrary, rightly directed meditation is indeed most fruitful, for it is the only true means whereby we can attain to a higher moral and spiritual development. It will be remembered that in the rough classification of complexes, given above, the final class was called the Great Complex; and in a note it was stated that the expression had been borrowed from the *Mahā-Sudassana-Sutanta*. It may be advisable at this stage to give a rather fuller account of this conception. The following quotation from Professor Rhys Davids's translation of the *Sutanta* well illustrates the meaning:

Now there occurred this thought to the Great King of Glory: "Of

what previous character, now, may this be the fruit, of what previous
character the result, that I am now so mighty and so great?'' And then
occurred to the Great King of Glory this thought: ''Of three qualities
is this the fruit, of three qualities the result, that I am now so mighty and
so great—that is to·say, of giving, of self-conquest, and of self-control!''

Now the Great King of Glory ascended up into the chamber of the
Great Complex; and he broke out into a cry of intense emotion:

> Stay here, O thoughts of lust!
> Stay here, O thoughts of ill-will!
> Stay here, O thoughts of hatred!
> Thus far only, O thoughts of lust!
> Thus far only, O thoughts of ill-will!
> Thus far only, O thoughts of hatred!

And when the Great King of Glory had entered the chamber of the
Great Complex, and had seated himself upon the couch of gold, having
put away all passion and all unrighteousness, he entered into, and remained in, the First Rapture,—a state of joy and ease, born of seclusion,
full of reflection, full of investigation.

.   .   .   .

By putting away ease, by putting away pain, by the previous doing
away both of gladness and of sorrow, he entered into, and remained in,
the Fourth Rapture,—a state of purified self-possession and equanimity,
without ease, and without pain.

At this point the translator adds the following note:

The above paragraphs are an endeavour to express the inmost feelings,
when they are first strung to the uttermost, by the intense effects of deep
religious emotion, and then feel the effects of what may be called, for
want of a better word, the reaction. Most deeply religious natures have
passed through such a crisis; and though the feelings are perhaps really
indescribable, this passage is dealing, not with a vain mockery, but with
a very real event in spiritual experience. It implies neither hypnotism
nor trance.

To continue and conclude our quotation, the extract proceeds:

Then the Great King of Glory went out from the Chamber of the
Great Complex, and entered the Golden Chamber and sat himself
down on the silver couch. And he let his mind pervade one quarter of
the world with thoughts of Love; and so the second quarter, and so the
third, and so the fourth. And thus the whole wide world, above, below,
around, and everywhere, did he continue to pervade with heart of

Love, far-reaching, grown great, and beyond measure, free from the least trace of anger or ill-will[1].

What it is exactly that people mean when they insist that a sound educational system should include the cultivation of the feelings as well as of the intellect, it would be difficult to say; for the growth of the feelings in one direction or another is inevitable. But vaguely, no doubt, the suggestion is that the mere acquisition by children of mental and manual skill, added to a familiarity with certain intellectual concepts, without however an awakening of lofty aspirations, sympathy and kindness of heart, is morally speaking unprofitable, and may be indeed a curse rather than a blessing.

Now whatever importance we may attach to the influence of heredity, and this factor should by no means be disregarded, it is quite certain that an individual's tastes, that is to say, his likes and dislikes, his aims and preferences, are not fixed and unchangeable elements, but that they are qualities which can, in special cases, be cultivated, repressed and developed practically without limit. It is, moreover, a well-established fact that an ordinary individual's tastes are dependent on his beliefs, perceptions and habitual modes of thought. In other words, he likes what he believes in; and also, in spite of his methods of "reasoning" (one might almost say in consequence of them), he is disposed to believe in the truth of what he likes. What we like and believe in, with some degree of persistence, are commonly called our "ideals."

It may be remarked in passing that this very generally recognised psychological fact, as to the interdependence of beliefs and wishes, is often dismissed with the phrase that "the wish is father to the thought" as a sufficient explanation. But it sometimes happens that the word "necessity" is used to express some attitudes of mind attuned to strong and deeply-rooted wishes or cravings, especially where such feelings synchronise with the

[1] *Sacred Books of the Buddhists,* Vol. III, pp. 218 and 219.

mental attitude of those with whom we have to deal. Thus we often speak of our "economic necessities" when we seek to give euphemistic expression to those settled mental habits, based upon desires and beliefs, to which we have merely grown accustomed. The cravings which have engendered certain habits of thought are in this manner made to appear to be of such compelling force as to suggest the idea of something fixed and irrevocable, springing out of the very essence of our nature, determining our actions "against our will" and contrary to our "interests." It will soon be made clear, however, that all our cravings are only relative and conditional, and that they should never, except by a misuse of terms, be spoken of as permanent or irresistible.

This brings us to the important and very difficult subject of instincts. The term "instinct" has been variously and inconsistently applied to a vast number of conflicting desires and proclivities, but generally to those more or less spontaneous tendencies, which prompt an organism's activities through the stimulus of environment towards the advancement, or maintenance, of its "well-being." Instinct has been aptly defined as the inborn experience of the race to which the organism belongs. But what is race-experience? Clearly it must be the outcome of an aggregate individual experience—a synthetic boiling down of innumerable efforts, trials, successes and failures.

However vast and profound this experience may be, it cannot approach infallibility, as the circumstances in which the organism finds itself placed can be varied practically without limit.

In the early part of this chapter we have seen that an essential element in the composition of complexes is experience; and it is obvious that the nucleus of all individual experience must be race-experience. In other words, a complex has its primary basis in instinct. Inasmuch, however, as the individual experience is ever widening and deepening, the instincts themselves must be ever changing in their incidence. They can consequently be modified and improved by individual effort, notwithstanding

Herbert Spencer's sage remark that "there is no political alchemy by which you can get golden conduct out of leaden instincts."

The most fundamental instinct is that which is known as the instinct of self-preservation. That little word "self" is responsible for much confusion of thought. Its ambiguity causes it to be allied to a number of conflicting ideas, but, in the main, it has opprobrious implications. Thus we speak of selfish, self-seeking, and self-absorbed; while in an opposite sense we applaud self-knowledge, self-control, self-culture, self-respect and self-reverence. Professor Huxley once pointed out that an evil effect of superficial education was due to confusion of thought which arose from the ambiguity of terms in current use, and argued that many imagined that they were well educated when they had merely learnt the art of stringing words together without associating with them any particular ideas.

In this connection the distinction between egoism and true individuality is of very great importance, and may help us to keep clear from the confusion which arises from the ambiguity of the word "self." The characteristic mark of egoism, then, is the mental seizing upon one's limitations, as though they were ultimate facts, a mere complex reaction in short, implying a futile endeavour in the direction of fixity and permanence in the phenomenal world; individuality, in contradistinction, implies, in its best sense, a continuity of higher effort in the direction of inward growth, expansion and unity. Those revelations of the real correlation of the forces underlying all phenomena which we have spoken of are a constant accompaniment of genuine individual growth. Such revelations, or true perceptions, have tremendous executive power as compared with the force of mere egoistic tendencies, with which they are generally in conflict, though their respective energies need not in practice be wholly incompatible with one another. The former agencies, being of a more spiritual nature, act synthetically and sympathetically; while the latter act by a process of exclusion. With an imperfect consciousness of individual spiritual effort, the painful emotions, which accompany nearly all such personal activities, may be said to *precede* joyous realization; with pronounced egoistic activity, on the contrary, painful feelings *follow* upon those transitory pleasures, which result in disillusionment or failure. Those illuminating ideas and perceptions are indeed the fundamental basis of all true modesty; but modesty must not be confused with timidity.

The word *egoistic*, as commonly employed, has almost inevitably some opprobrious implication; but one should be on one's guard against using it indiscriminately to describe an individual. In the French language, egoism is a term of abuse, synonymous with our *selfishness*. It means not only self-love, but a disregard for others. Similarly in recent pseudo-scientific writings we find numerous references to *narcissism*, derived from the myth of Narcissus, who fell in love with his own image. This and other terms intended to avoid the ambiguity of *self*, and to give a general air of terminological precision, are supposed to indicate a perversion of individuality. As we all know, almost any individual can appear egoistic on certain occasions; but this appearance merely implies that there are, in his composition, various complexes or constellations, which emerging dissociatively, impart to that individual, for the time being, a petty aspect, whether it takes the form of vanity, boastfulness, a pretentious self-sufficiency, jealousy, meanness, or malice. The same individual on other occasions may be generous, upright, tolerant and self-sacrificing. Now observing such manifestations of contradictory characteristics, critics are tempted to inquire which is the "real self," the "egoistic" or the "altruistic." The obvious answer afforded by a little reflection is that the "real self" is a myth. Individuality is comprehensively the whole life in diversified albeit causal continuity. This continuity, according to circumstance, sometimes appears discordant, at other times concordant, rhythmical and symmetrical. The estimate of an individual's character made by friends or acquaintances is, as a rule, quite superficial and untrustworthy. Some take people as they find them, others judge them by repute; the majority do both indiscriminately. The essential matter for our immediate consideration is that few have anything more than a very imperfect acquaintance with their own individuality; and that in ordinary practice we experience very great difficulty in acquiring the rudiments of self-knowledge.

To return now to the instinct of self-preservation. It will at once be seen that its tendencies and activities may vary according to whether it is acting upon the organism from a higher or lower plane of evolution—whether, that is to say, its energies are directed towards preserving the physical organism merely, or promoting the spiritual growth of the individual. This differentiation of instinctive feeling gives rise to a conflict among the complexes; and all conflict is painful.

Attempts to draw a hard and fast line of demarcation between "instinctive" and "volitional" actions are futile. Long established actions and reflexes in our various organs, the functioning of which is unaccompanied by any critical awareness of their purpose, may conveniently be called instinctive; while those accompanied by such awareness, and operating, more or less, according to a certain consciousness of selection and choice, may conveniently be called volitional. In so far as human beings are concerned, this is no more than a rough and ready classification, seeing that in actual life the two classes merge the one into the other. So likewise the differentiation of muscular activity into "voluntary" and "involuntary" may be regarded as a useful generalization, though without finality. Much light has been thrown on this subject by the recent researches of Dr Cannon and his associates. These researches are carefully recorded in that very valuable work: *Bodily Changes in Pain, Fear, Hunger and Rage.* It is there demonstrated that the secretions of the adrenal glands, caused by strong emotions, have the effect of suspending the functions of the "involuntary" or "sympathetic" nervous system, while at the same time they augment the powers of the "voluntary" or central system. This stimulation of the adrenals by emotional shock, and the persistence of that stimulation through complex dissociation, explain, in great measure, some of the hitherto mysterious phenomena of hysterical paralysis and other functional disorders whether respiratory or alimentary.

The conclusion which we draw from these reflections is that the only real *remedy* for human pain, as distinguished from temporary palliatives, is such systematic education as will effectively subordinate our lower to our higher purpose. This may be called a truism; but the study of the conclusions of psychology, or more correctly of psycho-physics, and their intelligent application to practical life, will help to keep its truth actively in view.

CHAPTER II

EMOTION AND INSTINCT

W E have seen that emotion is an essential element in the formation of complexes. Let us endeavour to elucidate the matter by means of concrete illustrations.

The ordinary human mind is a crowded aggregation of incipient beliefs, mental habits, concepts, longings and aversions, for the most part instinctive—mere potentialities. There is no such thing as an empty mind; nor is there any unchanging mind. These beliefs and tendencies are necessarily correlated, and, as the individual life develops, they fluctuate, mingle and conflict.

A proposition presenting itself for consideration, either at the instance of outward circumstances, or as the result of meditations, is accepted as true, or is rejected as false, with varying degrees of hesitation, according to our moods. If the proposition appeals to us as decidedly advantageous, that is to say, if it seems to open up the prospect of pleasurable emotion, and if it be not in strong disagreement with some particular habit of thought at the time active, the tendency of the mind is to accept such a proposition as a true pronouncement. Its unpleasantness, on the contrary, at once prompts its rejection. There are exceptions to the latter course in the case of so-called timid natures, whose egoism takes the form of credulity or over-suggestibility, coupled with a morbid apprehension of any invasion of the sanctity of their personality: but this exception does not affect the general rule.

Let the proposition, for example, be related to Art, some question of architectural style, a scheme of decoration, the quality or disposition of furniture: we call it a matter of good or of bad taste, according to our predilections. Let us suppose that it is a political question, or one of literature, science, or religion, and that it forms the topic of discussion with acquaintances. If now it should happen that the question is one which excites in us strong feelings, then agreement stimulates mutual interest and sympathy between individuals, apparently irrespective of the real character and essential merits of the subject discussed. The tendency also is towards hasty and unwarranted generalization. We are apt to call the people who are in accord with us, nice people, interesting and well-informed: those who differ from us are ignorant and evilly-disposed. Furthermore, when a proposition is supposed to correspond with what we imagine to be the universal experience of our fellows, tested by observation and accepted on authority, we call it "objective truth." Thus in former days the revolution of the sun and stars round the earth, as centre of the universe, was an obvious "fact," an "objective truth": and Galileo for holding contrary views was considered an enemy of the human race.

The contention here is not that there are no trustworthy criteria for distinguishing right from wrong, what is true from what is false, but that they do not exist wholly apart from the processes of mind, of which the emotional quality is an important factor in their growth and determination. In other words, human judgment is necessarily related to temporal conditions and at its best it is neither absolute nor final. It is noticeable that mere certitude is with many, particularly the young, accepted for the moment as a sure test of truth, until experience teaches them that one can feel quite certain about something, which turns out to be erroneous.

However much we may insist, as we often do, that we are quite impartial in our judgments, and however near some may approach to that ideal, yet it can hardly be gainsaid that, in practical life, impartiality is never to be counted on.

Many years ago John Stuart Mill argued with great force that all our accepted rules dealing with the idea of justice and fair play were mere human conventions based upon established

beliefs of very slight permanent validity. Such conventions have
their value, no doubt, in giving expression to prevalent beliefs;
they help men to co-operate, by reminding them of their mutual
obligations. But no sensible person to-day would insist that any
convention, although it may be embodied in the law of the land,
must be regarded as absolutely fixed and irrevocable. Trouble
inevitably arises when sections of the community, having lost
faith in the authority of certain conventions, find themselves in
conflict with the law, while at the same time other sections
insist upon the sacredness of the law, as an embodiment of
eternal truth. More especially is this the case when, as often
happens, the same individuals or groups accept conflicting conventions with almost equal fervour.

The organised life of civilised states has developed rapidly, and
it has certainly become very complicated, but all the elaborate
machinery set up by democracies for the readjustment of laws
by means of legislation, and for the alteration of the *personnel*
of administration, appears to be still quite inadequate to cope with
the very numerous manifestations of discontent. The demands
made in divers quarters for the greater satisfaction of "natural
rights" are becoming daily more insistent. On all sides the cry
is the same: "All we ask for is justice"; and few there are who
suspect that the only real satisfaction comes from within.

Shakespeare's play *The Merchant of Venice* was evidently
written with the object of bringing home to the average intelligence the great truth that "laws" must be harmonised to conform with mercy; and it is rather curious to note, that notwithstanding our professedly great admiration for Shakespeare, what
a confused kind of controversy is invariably provoked by the
occasional revival of public presentations of this play.

The spirit of unrest, which at present prevails in all departments of our communal life, both in thought and practice, seems
to call loudly for the awakening of some higher faith in the
purpose and destiny of individual existence; and how is this

possible without a serious effort being made to introduce a really moral and religious atmosphere into popular education? For it is difficult to see how all this confusion in our intellectual standards of value can by any possibility be resolved, so long as the egoistic and emotional character of the human mind remains undisciplined and rampant. When, however, the energies of our emotions are subdued or sublimated by alliance with higher ideals, then there is more elasticity and free play between the minor complexes, less danger of their dissociative emergence into consciousness, and as a consequence a clearance of the field for the exercise of our higher powers of perception and understanding.

We have seen that it is instinct which is the foundation and origin of the complexes; and that instinct has a twofold function: first the development, preservation and reproduction of the physical organism, as an individual organism: secondly the evolution of this organism as an instrument or vehicle of the higher purpose of the race to which it belongs. These two functions may operate harmoniously together; or they may act, if undue stress is laid on one or the other function, in apparent conflict.

Activity due to instinct is generally speaking either pleasurable or painful, according to its direction—whether that direction be positive or negative. It is directed positively in the exercise of the nutritive and reproductive functions of our bodies, in the development of the various senses and organs of the body, and in the development of the intellectual and moral qualities. It is directed negatively when it manifests itself as warnings and pains, which arise from the apprehension of dangers, either physical, intellectual, or moral, such as occur in the form of disease, or in the form of violent shocks to the system. The correct interpretation of instinctive feelings is, therefore, of the highest importance to our welfare; and it follows that we should endeavour as early as possible to supplement the instinctive tendencies of our nature by the cultivation of intelligent volitions, and by the stimulation of the habit of rapidly forming sound judgments in difficult situations. If we allow mere pleasurable sensations to prompt our thoughts and actions, thus using what intellectual powers we may first acquire towards the gratification of instinctive desires, our instincts themselves become perverted. Such perversion is unfortunately only too common. We see the wholesome appetite for food rapidly degenerate into gluttony. We see the instincts of self-preservation, of sense development, of reproduction and of intellectual growth perverted into luxurious living, aesthetic sensuality, lust and vanity.

A great danger lurks in the oft-repeated saying: "Let us enjoy ourselves while we are young and when we can." There is fortunately a happy mean which lies between the extreme of asceticism, of puritanical notions which regard all enjoyment as sinful, on the one hand; and of the opposite extreme, the short-sighted hedonism of mere pleasure-seeking, on the other.

The reaction against repression, as an educational ideal, seems to have gone quite far enough, so that we are now confronted with some very extravagant claims as to the "rights of children." Many are apt now-a-days to lose sight of the important fact that habits, growing out of the unrestrained vent given to instinctive feelings in youth, are likely to become very stubborn barriers to the individual's higher intellectual and moral growth. These habits tend towards the production of a multitude of irrational and superstitious beliefs, fancies, false and exaggerated expectations. Vague notions of "luck" and "chance" fill the thoughts with an inevitable train of disappointments, resentments and bitterness.

If all instincts were directed simply towards the preservation, development and reproduction of the physical organism, without regard to any higher human purpose, then indeed the continuity of mankind as a manifestation of spiritual life would be impossible. As a fact, however, there are instinctive energies continually exerting themselves throughout the various phases of our intellectual and moral growth; and inasmuch as the healthy development of this growth involves the harmonious interaction, mutually conscious and volitional, between different individual lives, too great importance cannot be attached to the intelligent co-ordination, sublimation and systematic training of instinctive feelings.

One of the most noticeable consequences of the neglect of such systematic training is to be seen in the mental habit of impatience with outward conditions, that exaggerated longing for the immediate emergence of tangible results from all efforts and actions; a longing which often finds expression in a futile and vulgar utilitarianism. Then again that narrow outlook upon life, engendered by strong feelings associated with an inadequate intellectual and moral equipment, leads to what is known as "cocksureness"—a distressing form of conceit impenetrable to pure reason. The immensity of the phenomenal world, with its balancing tendencies of innumerable conflicting influences, is disputed or ignored; and the pain, which follows disillusionment, finds its vent in pessimism, or in the preposterous doctrine called the "philosophy of discontent."

But patience is not apathy. Energies well directed, first within and then without, lead to lasting results; and unsought for though they be in their outward aspect, their fruit is the growth of a noble character.

CHAPTER III

CHARACTER VERSUS REPUTATION

ARE character and reputation necessarily in opposition to one another? The answer to this question must depend, as in all verbal propositions, on the implication of the words used.

Shakespeare makes Iago say to Othello:

> Good name, in man or woman, dear my lord,
> Is the immediate jewel of their souls:
> Who steals my purse steals trash; 'tis something, nothing;
> 'Twas mine, 'tis his, and has been slave to thousands;
> But he who filches from me my good name,
> Robs me of that, which not enriches him,
> And makes me poor indeed.

This is a striking passage and is often quoted, but, if carefully analysed, it soon becomes apparent that neither from a legal, economic, nor from an ethical point of view is it at all sound. Moreover on another occasion the same worthy says to Cassio: "Reputation is an idle and most false imposition; oft got without merit, and lost without deserving." Now Iago was a clever rascal of good repute, who did not, as a rule, say things with a view to helping his fellow-creatures to arrive at a better understanding of what was true; and in both the above citations he was endeavouring to mislead by specious and fallacious utterances. Good name and good reputation are synonymous; but they do not invariably tally with good character. The character of an individual is his actual nature, his true qualities, his tastes, capacities and disposition, his limitations, what he aims at becoming and the efforts he makes towards the attainment of his ideals; his reputation is the recorded or otherwise expressed opinions, or beliefs, which are generally held in regard to him and his works. There may be much coincidence between reputation and character, but it need not necessarily be so. Both have their proper uses in their respective spheres. It will, however, be very generally conceded as being quite obvious that character, as an aim, and as a determining factor in mankind's well-being, is of immeasurably greater importance than mere reputation. Very generally conceded, that is to say, by those who will pause to reflect; for it must be admitted that the opposite view prevails largely in our practical work-a-day life.

How does the confusion arise? In the first place it is held, and quite properly, that we can only judge of results, unless indeed we are endowed with super-normal faculties, which, as a rule, we do not possess. Thus the habit grows of looking for *results* and endeavouring to obtain them, not as a means of forming sound judgments as to the meaning and purpose of life, but as constituting in themselves the true use and goal of our existence. It is, then, just this inversion of the proper relations of the inward and outward, of means and end, that is responsible for the pernicious custom, widely prevalent, of neglecting, not to say ignoring, the importance of character-training.

One of the worst consequences of this exaggerated regard for reputation is the constant struggle to *appear consistent* and to gain, by one trick or another, some of the *outward marks* of virtue, ability, distinction, refinement and credibility, rather than to make the effort to develop the higher qualities in themselves[1]. Thus as civilization advances and the complications of life grow greater, we are confronted with the most deplorable waste of human energy in the vain attempt of individuals, groups, classes and nations to maintain their position in the eyes of the world; a struggle which manifests itself in that great mass of affectation and vulgar display; and in those varieties of fraud, folly and make-believe, which we all see and deplore, but fail adequately to cope with. It is important to note, however, that this exaggerated and topsy-turvy attitude towards the relative positions of character and reputation does not necessitate either the repudiation, nor

[1] See also Chapter VIII.

even the disregard, of one or the other. It is a question solely
of the view we take of their relative positions. The point is:
which shall be predominant; which is to be subordinated and
which is to be considered supreme? For undoubtedly a due regard
to reputation has its value in the regulation of our lives. It is
a form of discipline which under present conditions cannot well
be dispensed with. It is a useful reminder, a test, or measure of
practical efficiency, and a strong, though an inferior, incentive
to honest effort.

A proper regard for one's reputation may act as a corrective
to those exaggerated feelings of *independence* and *self-sufficiency*
which sometimes prompt young people into irrational attempts
at *self-assertion* and *self-justification*. Thus also the care for
reputation may help to remind us of the importance we attach
to hostile opinions regarding our conduct or attainments. It is
not uncommon, for example, to hear people protest that they
do not care in the least for what others say or think of them;
without, in fact, having any genuine, or enduring, belief in the
truth of their protestation. This reckless pretence that one is
always following the dictates of "conscience" when, in truth,
the actual prompter is some egoistic delusion, whether it be
called vanity or ill-temper, tends by constant repetition to destroy
the sense of shame which is a very powerful moral force.

The larger question of our relative *dependence, independence*
and *interdependence* will be dealt with more fully later on.

The difficulty of the educational problem, which presents
itself when we endeavour to inculcate the superiority of character
to reputation, lies in the fact that the early stages of child-
development depend so largely upon the feeding and cultivation
of the minor complexes, in which narrow egocentric thoughts
and feelings must necessarily predominate. The problem then
assumes this form: how are we to counteract these budding and
multifarious egoisms in the minor complexes without destroying
all incentives to effort? This problem is the subject of the next
chapter.

CHAPTER IV

INCENTIVES TO EFFORT. ECONOMICS

W
E exert ourselves to obtain pleasure and to avoid pain; to reach out towards what attracts, and to escape from what repels. Experience teaches us what is good for us. Thus stated the question of our incentives appears simple enough. But in reality it is not so.

A child sees something that looks good, or smells good, and so thrusts it into his mouth. He may find it bitter, or too hot—not at all what he expected. Grown-up people likewise are deceived by their senses, by their opinions, by their false inferences and expectations. What is learnt by experience one day may have to be unlearnt the next. Further, similar objects may appear attractive at one time and repellent at another. Even at the same moment we may be both attracted and repelled by the same, or what appears to be the same, course of action by different sides of our nature, in short by different complexes.

It is true, of course, that certain customs and beliefs have gained general acceptance as a result partly of transitory experience and partly of tradition.

Let us examine some of these accepted beliefs. Physical and mental enjoyment, arising from the exercise of the senses, bodily exercise, rational intellectual pursuits and diversions, which meet with approbation, applause, or "legitimate success," and which result in personal advancement in the eyes of the world; a life, in short, of distinction, pleasure or ease; any or all of these aims are, by tacit consent, recognised as worthy objects of existence, and advantageous, not to say necessary, incentives to effort. The making of adequate provisions for securing and perpetuating such obviously good things is called foresight, prudence, common sense. Yet, strange to say, we can, in certain moods, admire far more the motives of those who systematically discard all such aims as these. In our higher moods the ordinary outlook upon life appears to us, not as common sense, but as commonplace, selfish and vulgar.

That beautiful word love is much used and abused in describing human motives. It is, in fact, associated with two distinct ideas having opposed tendencies. Correctly it is used to denote that expansive force in our nature which arises out of a surrender of egoistic thoughts and feelings; but it is also used, though often with the implication of the ironic colloquialism *cupboard-love*, as applying to the extension of our egoism, allied to the sense of property and possession. In this sense it would more properly be termed affection. In its best meaning, love is indicative of the highest religious emotion, not the mere profession of a creed, nor mere devotion to ceremonial observances, but as indicating reverence for the eternally true and the divinely beautiful in both man and nature. In the other sense, love implies a mere attachment to our belongings, or would-be possessions, such as our homes, families, friends. Thus an individual says he loves, when he speaks of the things that are particularly *his*, or the things he would like to *have*. He says:—I love *my* home (or *our* home), *my* family, *my* friends, *my* art, *my* country, *my* religion. These objects may certainly be shared with others, but mixed with the idea of exclusion and proprietorship. This is not true love, but affection. It is only when the egoistic feeling is in abeyance that we can truly be said to love. Then indeed we see life in its proper perspective. We are then able to perceive that the basis upon which the great bulk of human motives rests is a sense of the absolute separateness of one individual from another and of one complex from another; that sense which arises from our deeply-rooted belief in our physical and psychic isolation. In that belief we develop most of our ideals, we seek our security, and we formulate our plans.

However much we may protest that this belief is delusive and misleading, its almost universal existence is a hard fact, a fact which has to be reckoned with and provided for, if we would deal with our fellow-men. What is more, an adequate understanding of its true meaning and implication, its force, scope and limitations, must be acquired before we can make serious progress in any attempt to remove its baneful influence by means of education.

It is to the sense of separateness that the economic fabric of our lives owes its rise. Economic systems at once emphasize the fact of its existence, and supply, though only partially and imperfectly, a means of escape. This sense of separateness, as it obtains in the ordinary human mind, is somewhat distorted, perverted, and, so to speak, uneducated. It tends to promote error of judgment in so far as it makes the temporary and conditional limits of perception appear absolute and final. It makes the mere spatial and transitory relationship of things appear absolutely fixed and complete. It obscures one of the most fundamental facts of life, for, whether we know it or not, we are necessarily interdependent, we must perforce co-operate with one another, however much we may hug the belief in our independence. Herein arises, by a process of inversion, a strange anomaly. We have come to regard *money*, the very instrument forged by long ages of civilization to unite our energies in productive activity, as the real basis of true independence; as indeed the only effective and honourable means of securing freedom in our lives.

It is often assumed, as a self-evident proposition, that finance is an absolutely essential factor in the production of life's necessaries. A moment's reflection would convince us how absurd the proposition is, for it does not require any great stretch of imagination to conceive the existence of a state of things in which human beings had learnt to co-operate spontaneously for their mutual aid, without requiring any cumbersome machinery for

measuring, checking and regulating their individual and collective
activities. History has, in fact, furnished us with examples of
such true community of interest and endeavour. One might
instance the building of some of our finest cathedrals. Even
to-day the best part of our social life has a non-economic basis.
We have, however, grown so much accustomed to look upon
the commercial side of life as being the most important, that
we often hear the financial aspect of a question presented as
a mark of finality. Thus it is much more polite to say we are
unable to afford compliance with some request than to say point-
blank that we do not wish to comply. The statement as to our
inability to afford any thing may be true or it may not, but
whether or not it is true, the excuse of financial incapacity is
accepted as valid, and is not generally thought impolite. One
does certainly meet with the opposite extreme, of people who
pretend to be better off than they are, and who affect complete
indifference to monetary considerations; but this attitude is not
nearly so popular, and is usually suspected. The suggestion is
not that we could forthwith dispense with our economic system,
or even that at this stage it would be advantageous. The point is,
that finance absorbs too much of our thoughts, and wrongly.
The economic sphere has become too dominant, too insistent;
it no longer occupies its proper place in our lives. The instrument, or servant, has become master.

Why is this? It is the outcome of that process of perversion,
or rather inversion, already referred to. Civilization has developed
very rapidly. The application of our minds to material considerations has, in proportion to our moral growth, been somewhat
overdone, and a systematic readjustment has become necessary.

Money is supposed to be a standard of "value" and a measure
of "value." Much has been written as to the meaning of value.
It is not, however, necessary to enter here into the technical
minutiae of economic science. From a psychological point of
view, value is the mental estimation of what appears to us good,

or desirable; but seeing that such estimation varies from time to time, both with the same individual according to his conditions and circumstances, and with the different individuals into whose lives we enter, it is evidently a bootless task to attempt to fix, or define, some measure of value so as to give it anything approaching to universal application. Money, no doubt, has its own function in its proper sphere, but the mistake we are constantly making is to try to measure by its means that with which it is altogether incommensurate.

The delusion that money is an universal power, meeting all human needs, is a superstition amounting almost to idolatry.

This money worship is no mere rhetorical figure of speech. We see its baneful effects in the attitude different sections of the community, who should be working harmoniously for their mutual good, are tending to adopt towards one another. We see one of its consequences in the perverted meaning now so often attached to the word "charity." Charity originally expressed the most ennobling quality of the human mind. Charity, which means properly kindness of heart, good will, mutual helpfulness and tolerance, has become almost synonymous with degradation. It is supposed to imply a contemptuous pity for incapacity and practical worthlessness, something that no self-respecting individual would care to be associated with, because of its demoralising influence upon its recipients. "We want work not charity" is a cry often heard from the unemployed, with approval and sympathetic applause. They demand their "rights." The owners of property, the representatives of privileged positions and vested interests are in the main responsible for this anomaly, for they have maintained and taught that they are the rightful dispensers of charity; and the "masses" have accepted these ideas from them. Thus the "workers" are losing sight of the fact that they too might be charitable, and in the true sense of the word. They are for the most part intensely self-righteous; though if their righteousness was genuine, they would, instead of parading their "ideals," recognise that those who have most need of their charity are just the benighted possessors of the "good things of this world." Instead of envying them, they would pity them, bearing in mind that the rich will hardly enter into the kingdom of heaven. But they do envy the "good things"; and as to the warning, they are prepared to take the risk. They imagine that, through the power of money, they can gain all the blessings of the rich. They seem quite incapable of understanding that what gives undue power to "moneyed classes" is just this stupid envy and admiration of the ignorant crowd. Indeed their veneration for money is so extreme, that they have come to believe that to work for it is not only necessary for their independence and healthful existence, but also that it is positively ennobling to the human mind. The "employers" labour under the same delusion. They too, as a whole, believe that the purpose of all industry, whether it be manufacturing, agricultural, or mercantile, is the successful accumulation of money; and that the supply of the public's wants is quite a secondary affair.

This is no exaggeration. It expresses a type of inversion that is so common, that with the great majority the mere fact of calling attention to its existence is supposed to be equivalent to arguing that money itself is useless or harmful. They seem as unable as children to grasp the fact that a tool is made and contrived for a specific use; and that it is dangerous to mishandle it. At the present time it is an undeniable fact that large sections of various distressed communities throughout the world, both employers and employed, are ardent advocates of the doctrine that the way to restore prosperity is to increase by some artifice the *scarcity* of the means whereby the community's wants are satisfied, so as to increase the abundance of the money available for distribution.

These are rough and general statements and should not, of course, be taken as excluding variations and exceptions; but the broad outline of *fact* is undoubtedly true, namely that money, being viewed as the prime source of power, comfort and security, is sought after and reverenced above everything else, as an end in itself. It is nevertheless true that if people are challenged on the point, and so made to think, they will almost always admit immediately that naturally money is only an instrument of exchange and a measure of market values. "We only require money for what we can buy with it; but at the same time it is a necessity of life, we could not do without it." They will generally insist too that they have got to get money "somehow," by fair means certainly, but they have got to get it. How much they have got to get is not explicitly stated, though we are led to infer that it is to be as much as possible. Such remarks are familiar enough, and are clear indications of dissociation. Certain of their complexes enable them to see the case correctly, while others, and it is to be feared more potent ones, see the matter *inverted*. They try to reconcile them with one another, and the result is what is known as a confusion of thought. When attempts are made to expose, in plain terms, this vulgar mental attitude, it assumes a grotesque appearance. There is what is called an "instinctive" revolt against these habitual modes of thought, but it is often extremely difficult to make the errors quite manifest. The dissociations are so liable to lead to a loss of temper. Still with perseverance and gentleness success is quite possible.

There are few more profitable educational fields than economics, for with the acquisition of sound views on the method which enables us to co-operate amicably for our mutual advantage, our whole character undergoes radical improvement. The question of *currency* is generally considered very difficult, not to say abstruse, but this belief arises out of the widespread ignorance of even the rudiments of economics. As a fact, currency problems are, at bottom, exceedingly simple. Questions of debased and inflated currency can be mastered even by children, provided they are properly taught. If more attention had been paid to such matters, it is more than probable that the Great War might have been avoided. When opposing parties differ from one another on matters that neither party can understand, it takes but few steps to advance towards the point where they are persuaded of each other's wickedness, followed by frantic demands for their mutual destruction.

Those moments in which we feel and perceive the underlying *oneness* of our lives are, it must be admitted, very rare. We do not at all times and in all circumstances realise our essential interdependence. Our whole natures have not yet acquired the capacity of giving and receiving freely. There is that in us, more especially as regards what we call our material interests, which *exacts* a *quid pro quo* for services rendered and "benefits" exchanged. It is our "dignity," we say, which demands it. Our "self-respect" requires it. Why, without such demand "we should be the prey to the idle, the greedy, the vicious." But that which really makes the demand is the innate egoism of our rudimentary natures, however much we may dress it up in high-sounding phrases. It is egoism which creates economic values just as certainly as it creates vice and greed and indolence.

Let us be clear about this before we endeavour to determine the remedy for our present ills.

Viewing the various social and political institutions of our times with honest and impartial judgment we cannot help seeing that they are all, more or less, built up on what is termed an economic basis. Whatever may be the superstructure, the foundation, or legal status, is one of "property," "endowment," and "contract." Religious, charitable, philanthropic, educational, industrial institutions, the institutions of marriage, of birth, of rank, of social procedure are all incorporated under the laws of contract relating to property, for privileged or exclusive use. Their dignity, prestige, honour, the measure of their freedom, power and stability are generally estimated in terms of money. Persons and institutions without property have "no stake in the country." Indeed with many people money has come to be regarded as a substitute for exertion, as the only true refuge and safeguard; even as a means of masking or concealing vice. Money is the power most admired, most respected, most coveted by the mass of mankind to-day, rich and poor alike, who are rapidly coming to consider that the "struggle for life" is a financial struggle, pure and simple.

That this should be the state of civilization in which we find ourselves placed is evidence of the way in which we have been brought up, and of the ideals under whose influence we have grown to be what we are. The facts need not be insisted on in any carping or malignant spirit, but if we would emancipate ourselves from this thraldom it must be boldly and frankly recognised.

If the question were propounded: are there no practical incentives to effort ranging between the extremes of narrow self-seeking, and the pursuit of the highest ideal? the answer should certainly be in the affirmative. In ordinary course it is of little use appealing to men, long addicted to the practice of money worship, to exercise forthwith the noblest human motives. There are occasionally cases of remarkable "conversion," but as a rule, there could be no satisfactory response to such an appeal. The appeal in general would be declared "impracticable," as unsuitable to a world animated, for the most part, by petty personal interests. It is nevertheless true that, apart from the vulgar love of gain, which may possibly be in temporary abeyance, obscured or disguised, there are, latent in most men, the motives of ambition, of a desire to triumph over practical difficulties, to show good results, to win the approbation and applause of their fellows. These are all potential motives deeply incorporated in our nature. These are motives which can be effectually appealed to. They are not certainly the highest motives, but attempts to ignore them, to decry them as vain and unworthy, for the vast majority, would prove quite futile.

Within a few weeks from the opening, on the 23rd of April, 1924, of the British Empire Exhibition at Wembley, a serious labour crisis arose in the grounds of the Exhibition. The greater number of those engaged on the work of construction laid down their tools, and made unreasonable demands for an increase of pay. These demands were not complied with, but instead an appeal was made to the workers' sense of duty, to their promises, to the importance of the tasks they had undertaken to fulfil, and to their interest in the work itself. This appeal prevailed; and within a few days of its being made, newspaper headlines announced: "Magical Changes at the Exhibition." "Wembley's Response to Call for Speeding up." "Twelve Days' Spurt." "Miracle of the Big Hustle." The following extract, from a leading journal, is typical of the statements appearing in the press of those days:

> Less than a fortnight ago it could have been said with perfect truth that to complete the British Empire Exhibition in time for the opening day was absolutely impossible, but now it can be said quite definitely that the Exhibition will be ready.
>
> Only those people who have had to take part in the gigantic activities that have been proceeding of late are able to understand adequately the set-backs of the last few weeks, and which are still being experienced on account of bad weather.
>
> But with many thousands of men, all actuated by the same impulse to complete—and willing now to work, when necessary, all through the night as well as the day—a dramatic change has taken place.

Making allowances for journalistic exuberance these statements were substantially correct.

The episode well illustrates the power of such appeals; and many similar might be quoted. It is a matter of stimulating dormant complexes, so that they may over-ride others that have become dominant. Some would prefer to speak of the "result of suggestion," or the "power of advertisement," but they amount to the same thing. The influence, however named, might be summed up as an appeal to *sentiment*, not, of course, in the perverted signification of "sentimental" (defined by the *Oxford Dictionary* as emotional weakness or mawkish tenderness). Properly, sentiment implies a respectful and sympathetic regard for the feelings and interests of our fellow-creatures in specific relationships. Many vague and ambiguous terms are used to express different sentiments, for example "honour," "efficiency," "emulation," "patriotism," "citizenship," "family pride," and the like. All these terms are liable to abuse, but they indicate aspects of our nature which certainly transcend the narrow egoisms displayed in the higgling of the market-place.

It is often stated, and with some truth, that in strict "business" there is little or no room for sentiment. The truth of the statement lies in the fact that it is of great importance to a community that those who engage in business (and practically all its members are, in one way or another, included under this head) should learn, both in their own interests and that of others, that they are required to keep their promises; and, what is almost of equal importance, that they must not recklessly make and exact promises. It should moreover be borne in mind that in business we are dealing with property, its rights and privileges; and with the mechanism for exchanging the ownership and benefits of property, according to the law. There is this further consideration, that in the laws of property and contract; and in the courts of justice which have grown up in all civilised states for the purpose of interpreting, administering and enforcing these laws; and in all the traditions of commercial life, there is a tacit recognition of egoistic or selfish motives as an essential factor in the determination of the legal "considerations" which form the basis of all *business transactions*. Yet at the same time it is an undoubted fact that, in industrial spheres of activity, there is a growing recognition of *interdependence* between various sections of the community. Certain factories and distributive organizations have been established in which the words co-operation and co-partnership have begun to be used, if somewhat vaguely. Such invidious expressions as "employer" and "employee" are discarded, and in their place we find substituted the more dignified and agreeable "co-partner" and "co-worker." Even customers or buyers are sometimes recognised as brethren, and cease to be regarded as awkward factors in the system who have to be cajoled, because they are at once necessary and antagonistic. Managers, foremen, skilled and unskilled artisans become a united proprietorship owing allegiance, one individual to another, in friendship and interest.

Amicable combinations like these seem to work well enough for a time, when, almost inevitably, the underlying defects of human nature begin to assert themselves. Greed, malice, jealousy, suspicion and ignorance become manifest, good feeling diminishes, ideals lose their hold on the imagination, and by degrees the whole fabric crumbles away.

Nevertheless these experiments are well worth attempting. They are educational object lessons, and they help, by a leavening process, to improve human nature itself. It is sometimes foolishly imagined that "co-operation" implies the denial or at least the ignoring of individuality. Indeed it is possible that it is through some confused thinking of this kind, that so many painstaking efforts at amicable co-operation have come to grief. Individuality for the great bulk of humanity includes, as a primal factor, the desire for personal protection, advancement and security. The denial of these desires, or an underestimation of their potency must invariably lead to trouble. It is in fact, not only necessary to acknowledge individuality, but it is for the very purpose of making a just apportionment of individual interests in practical co-operation, that monetary systems have had to be invented. As already indicated above, there is much popular misconception on questions relating to money and currency. It has become the fashion in certain quarters to insist that because money is an instrument for the exchange of commodities, it need not and should not itself have any intrinsic value. This is sheer nonsense.

Money is an instrument of exchange because it is also a measure of market values. It represents some specific value of portable property, or, in the case of credit, some well-certified promise to deliver that property, or its equivalent, in an agreed manner. All known forms of money are good, provided there is nothing equivocal as to the genuineness of the property they purport to represent, or the validity of the promises to hand it over. The term *currency* is commonly used as the equivalent of *legal tender*, i.e., that form of money a creditor is bound by law to accept in payment of a debt. In this country we now have the £1 *treasury note* as legal tender. It is "issued by the Lords Commissioners of His Majesty's Treasury under the Authority of Act of Parliament IV and V Geo. V, ch. XIV." This Act sets out that the holder of a £1 note is entitled to demand, in exchange for the note, one *sovereign*, a coin which by law is made of 123 grains of gold of 22 carats fineness. The reason why the £1 treasury note is not worth that amount of gold in the market is due to the fact that the free exportation of *sovereigns* is at the present time prohibited. The value of the note depends, therefore, on the degree of likelihood of the prohibitions being removed, and a free market in gold being restored. The chief reasons for the usefulness of gold as the basis of money are first, its comparative scarcity, and second, the almost universal desire of mankind to possess it. If gold were to become much more abundant than it is now, it would cease to be as serviceable as it is for the purpose.

These simple facts are well known to all those who have taken the trouble to inform themselves; and if they were more widely known much misery and discontent would be avoided.

The ambiguity of the term "wealth" is a serious difficulty, for it has a strictly limited signification in the sphere of economics, and it is used in a far wider sense in general literature and poetry and also colloquially. In its technical meaning, wealth is that which can be recognised by law as property, either personal, or collective, which can, therefore, be made the subject of bargain

P

and contract and which has in consequence an "exchange value."
Beneficence, in a spiritual sense, is in no way involved in the
conception of economic wealth, any more than the idea of true
self-sacrifice can be involved in the motives of economic gain.
The power of spiritual beneficence is, no doubt, stupendous in
its own sphere in the determination of human welfare, but it
belongs to a stratum of thought and action fundamentally
distinct from that covered by the world of economics. In our
dealings with one another these two strata may indeed seem to
be inextricably mixed up, but with the help of a higher insight
they can be distinguished, and if we are wise we should endeavour
to avoid all unnecessary confusion between them. Services
rendered from motives of true love, services rendered with the
spontaneous feeling and conviction that all our truest interests
and ultimate ends cannot be in any sense opposed, is essentially
free service. Such service is altogether unlike a business trans-
action, for it is not something which can be bought and sold.
We are, fortunately, most of us aware, in some parts of our lives,
that humanity is capable of acts of true kindness; and we know
that, while such acts generally inspire a kind of reciprocity both
in substance and feeling, they involve no definite provision for
any return in the nature of a stipulated "consideration," or
quid pro quo. In legal parlance they are "acts of grace," which
cannot be made the subject of litigation for the enforcement
either of benefits, or pains and penalties.

The aims of commerce, as commerce, are those of self-preservation and self-gratification, both in a very narrow sense; and self-
aggrandisement, in a worldly sense: that is, strictly personal, or
for our belongings. The methods of commerce are those of
strenuous competition.

If we concentrate our energies upon commercial pursuits and
deliberately adopt their methods, aims and ideals, as our own,
making them the dominant purpose and mainspring of our lives,
to the neglect or subordination of our spiritual capacities and
potentialities, we can, beyond doubt, achieve a certain kind of

temporal success. But the spiritual side of our nature will not for ever be denied. Some crisis will arise, whether it takes the form of disease, disaster, or death, which will find us unprepared, and shatter the fabric we have made. This is no mere hypothesis, but the universal experience.

It is often urged that the two sides of our nature can be made to work hand in hand. Possibly, but the important question is: which shall be dominant? Unless we constantly keep our minds clear on this point, the risk is very great. It is easy enough to say, as many do, that we will first make our worldly position secure, and then use the vantage ground, so gained, to "do good" afterwards. A strenuous commercial life, as things are to-day, is not the best school for learning the nature of good, or high moral purpose. Many there are who learn too late that there is truth in the warning that one cannot serve both God and Mammon.

The real remedy for our ills is to be found, and found solely, in sound educational methods; and this is not possible without knowledge of the composition and working of the human mind. This knowledge must in the first instance be gained by teachers, and it must be skilfully and fearlessly applied in practice.

We have seen that, by enlarging the field of vision and consciousness, complexes can be united, resolved and co-ordinated, so extending and purifying the sphere of experience and volition, and that the real strength and greatness of individuality lie in the direction of the impersonal. These are fundamental facts handed down to us by the noblest traditions and confirmed by experimental psychological research.

The genuine understanding of these fundamental facts would lead to the remodelling and readjustment of our whole educational system. Competition, in contradistinction to emulation, as an incentive to effort (and incidentally as the great fostering cause of egoism) would be abolished. Punishment would be mitigated. Bribes would disappear. Children would be discouraged from assimilating false ideals while their minds are young and plastic. Noble ideals would be placed before them and we should contrive and continue, by suitable examples and illustrations, to make these appear really interesting and attractive. Ideals so instilled tend to develop spontaneity of action; in a sense they become instinctive[1] and would have vastly greater weight and influence over life and conduct than mere intellectual concepts acquired later in life.

These higher instinctive aims, thoughts and feelings, ever seeking their expression in action, would, as life continues, extend their scope, strengthen their energies, and bring each individuality into more harmonious communion with other individualities, and with the outer world. The truer the instincts, the more real becomes the growth of the individuality in the direction of the impersonal.

In the incompletely developed mind, the field of vivid consciousness being necessarily narrow and circumscribed, a vast number of life's operations must pertain to the instinctive order. These are what have been termed "automatisms." In using this term it is important to bear in mind that such instinctive acts are by no means removed from all element of responsibility. It is true, no doubt, that automatisms, while functioning, have the effect of committing the individual without his having been fully aware of what he was about. Inasmuch, however, as they were the outcome of some, it may be, innumerable conscious efforts, or musings, they must be regarded as being in fact the deferred consequences of previous volitional activity. These considerations add point to the insistence upon the value of scientific study to the healthful and systematic governance of our lives. With a proper understanding of the laws of complex formation, and of the laws which regulate their interdependence, emergence and co-ordination, a great diminution could be effected in human suffering and worry. By means of such understanding we could substitute comparatively simple and direct methods for the cumbersome experiments, failures and false inferences characteristic of the ordinary processes of social evolution.

[1] See Chapters I and II.

CHAPTER V

SPECIALIZATION

THE innumerable divisions and subdivisions in the organised life of a community render some kind of specialization as regards instruction and training a virtual necessity. The various departments of State, the division of labour in productive and distributive enterprise, the growth and differentiation of professional occupations, of scientific research and recreative pursuits, all these tend to create an imperative demand for specially equipped and efficient workers, and as a consequence for "vocational training."

In recent years specialization has grown very fast and has already produced surprising results; but carried to extremes it has very serious drawbacks. For it has the effect of narrowing down the individual outlook and of isolating, or dissociating, the component parts of the social organism with the result that efficiency is, on the whole, not gained, but lost. The pernicious craze for "record breaking"; that extravagant longing to achieve something striking, or sensational, something that will "stir the public mind" to admiration and applause, fosters a most unwholesome influence in our midst. The concentration of people's thoughts and imagination upon the ephemeral data of outward events, as though these constituted in themselves the object and goal of existence, must tend to divert attention from really important matters, to distort and confuse our sense of proportion, and make us lose sight of what is fundamentally essential to our welfare and true progress.

Not so very long ago it was very commonly held that by a vigorous application of the mind to no matter what subject, one could thereby develop certain important "faculties," which were called "*the* will," "*the* memory," "*the* power of concentration," and "*the* power of observation"; and that once gained these "faculties" could be applied to any and all purposes! Modern physiological and psychological research[1] has utterly exploded this doctrine. Scientific research clearly indicates that observation, memory, concentration and volition are developed only in conjunction with specific ideas, emotions and actions; that the development of these mental powers, along certain lines, involves the development of specific functions of the brain and nervous system acting in combination with various organs, more especially the ductless glands; and that, for the higher purposes of our communal life, or for any purpose other than those so specifically developed, these awakened powers of the mind are quite useless; unless, indeed, there is an adequate extension of the associative or assimilative processes, linking the specific complexes, so formed, with other complexes, especially with the more general or co-ordinating complexes.

An uneducated farmer, calling at a country house to obtain the signature of a local magnate to some document, was asked to wait in the library. He afterwards expressed to a friend his astonishment at the large number of "Bibles," which he had "observed," stored up on the shelves. The Family Bible was the only book with which he was familiar and it happened to have an outward resemblance to the books in the library. Hence his inference as the outcome of his "observations." But let the owner of the library, the educated man of affairs, quite uninstructed in practical agricultural operations, walk the fields with this man of the soil, and the tables would be turned; all his widely cultivated and scholarly powers of observation would serve him but little, and it is not unlikely that he would make just as foolish observations as that of the uncultured farmer. So

[1] See *Integrative Action of the Nervous System* by C. S. Sherrington, P.R.S., etc.; *Speech and Cerebral Localization* by Henry Head, M.D., F.R.S.; and Janet's *Major Symptoms of Hysteria*.

it is in other fields: observation, knowledge, volition are linked with the memory of what is familiar.

"Familiarity breeds contempt" expresses only a half-truth, for familiarity also breeds affection and interest. But it is true that phenomena familiar to an expert, a specialist, may seem utterly commonplace to him and to his fellow-experts, while to a non-expert, or to an expert in another line, the same phenomena may appear to be very wonderful and mysterious, so long as they are still unfamiliar.

It is difficult, no doubt, but few things are more important in education than to bear in mind, and to inculcate, the changing nature of everything and everybody. There are conceivably different kinds of duration as well as degrees of time corresponding to our various physical and psychical phases, but nothing is absolutely static; everything is related, conditioned and transitory. The nearest approach we can make to fixity and permanence is to be found in our enunciation of fundamental principles, or laws; nevertheless, even here it must not be forgotten that such enunciations are themselves dependent on our powers of expression and understanding; by no means immutable factors.

The common practice of labelling men according to their chief avocations is responsible for much unnecessary confusion; and it is sometimes a serious bar to our estimation of the real worth of an individual. We often hear such contemptuous exclamations as: "What can a lawyer know about farming?" "How can a doctor make a good man of business?" "Let the shoemaker stick to his last," and the like—the idea being that competence in one special line must necessarily involve disqualification for proficiency in other directions. Generalizations of this sort are just as misleading, in their own way, as their opposite extremes, to which reference has just been made. For they leave out of account a very valuable human quality, namely versatility, which, though often spoken of disparagingly, is essential to good citizenship. It has frequently been noticed how a first-rate lawyer, a highly skilled journalist, or a prominent statesman can, by strenuous application and a short term of study, become thoroughly expert in almost any branch of knowledge.

True versatility is acquired by the harmonization and drastic subjugation of the emotional element in most complexes. A versatile individual is one who has, in his own person, exemplified the process of co-ordination, whereby his higher complexes are developed.

CHAPTER VI

MULTIPLEX ENVIRONMENT

THE mental habit of differentiating all life's experiences into "subject" and "object," of drawing a rigid line of demarcation between these mental products, and of calling the object the "reality"—the "actual fact," as distinguished from what is supposed to represent merely transitory subjective states—is a habit which has become so deeply ingrained in the human mind, that it is difficult now-a-days to induce anyone seriously to consider a question from a different point of view. Indeed it is this deeply ingrained mental habit, with all its definitions, categories and other conventions, which forms the basis of the "exact sciences." Yet philosophically trained thinkers insist that our knowledge of matter and its qualities, our conceptions of time, space and motion, all in short that we believe concerning life, growth, form and substance, is reducible to more or less systematised mental phases, or concepts, arising out of "subject" perceptions.

It is true, no doubt, that our general powers of observation lead us to infer that every living organism is capable of experiencing such definite recurrences of psycho-physical phases[1] with such regularity and persistency as to indicate seemingly the existence of an "environment" independent of the organism itself. We cannot properly be said to *know* the existence of anything beyond our mental states or phases. We know, in other words, the occurrence of phenomena, and we infer the laws of their relation and causation, but we do not know of their independent existence.

[1] It should be noted here that the phrase "psycho-physical phase" used above does not necessarily involve such individualised developments as *consciousness* or *perception*.

It is particularly important to be clear on this point, because the term *phenomenon* is now frequently used, not in its proper philosophical signification of an *appearance*, but as the equivalent of *reality*, of "the objective truth."

"The truth" is, indeed, an expression very commonly employed, though improperly. Truth is an abstraction, the discovery of which can, in a sense, be aimed at. That which we actually *find*, and which we can properly be said to *know*, is the *true*, the relation between various psycho-physical phases.

The word *know* is here used in a somewhat restricted signification, as implying an actual awareness of specific things. Undoubtedly the word is often used loosely as a substitute for *believe, infer, surmise*, and sometimes even for *fancy* or *imagine*. Such words properly denote cognitive phases of mind, involving the recollection of matters of which we believe we have had or may have knowledge, but may have partially forgotten or lost sight of; things in short of which we are not fully and properly *aware*. Similarly, the words *real* and *reality* are ambiguous, being used sometimes merely to denote actualities in duration or time, supposed to exist apart from thought; and sometimes as the mere antithesis of false or sham. This loose and question-begging terminology represents a bad linguistic habit, having important bearings on the problems of veracity.

What, then, we do, when we have phenomena under observation, is to differentiate or polarise experience in accordance with well-established mental habits, and under the operation of more or less ascertainable laws of causation in mind. Individual observers, however, are not isolated, and they can, in varying degrees, share each other's experiences. It is this all-important fact which is the true inwardness of the Christian saying: "We are members one of another." To use the term *mind*, in its broad signification, is to designate that power or principle which is common to all existence. Mind does not exist solely in its transitory manifestations as consciousness and perception. It is the cause of manifestation of all that is, whether we call it animate or inanimate, material or spiritual. It is the basis of all experience. The ordinary individualised mind is partly "unconscious," latent, undifferentiated; the rest is either "conscious" or "subconscious," in extent or proportion respectively, according to the individual's development, qualities and circumstance. There are, of course, as we have seen, varying kinds and degrees of the conscious and the subconscious, but what we are concerned with at the moment is the fact that a great region of mind is neither conscious nor subconscious, but still is mind potentially, and the existence of which is actually felt when we engage in the operation of observing or cogitating upon fresh phenomena. Thus "environments" are aspects of mind varying indefinitely according to their observers, whether individual or collective, according, that is to say, to the experiences through which they are evoked. There are three kinds of environment corresponding to specific experiences. These are: (1) the environment due to unconscious mind, unassimilated to individualised life and practically universal; (2) the environment due to the diffused subconscious mentality of collective observers, which corresponds to the "Zeitgeist," "Herd instinct," clannishness, war and money worship; it is from this kind of environment that fashions, customs, conventions and concepts have their rise; (3) the environment due to the vivid waking of consciousness of individual observers.

The most truly valuable of all experiences are those where all three kinds of environment are evoked, or manifest themselves, harmoniously together—that is to say, when consciousness is, so to speak, focused concentrically through them all. This form of experience is, generally speaking, the outcome of perfect health and sanity.

Once these fundamental conceptions are grasped by the reader, he can extend, apply and illustrate their meaning by reference to his own personal experiences.

It might be objected, perhaps, that all personal experience implies the pre-existence of a separate subject or self. This objection is nothing more than a reassertion of the determined habit of differentiating all experience into subject and object. That this habit prevails is not now in question, and there is no immediate dispute as to its fundamental importance to individual existence; but the formulation of such an objection, in a philosophical discussion, indicates the obtrusion of what may be termed an intellectual complex of a pronounced egoistic type. The formation of such complexes is one of our chief difficulties, for they may be strongly emotional as well as intellectual, and they constitute serious bars to healthy mental development. If they do not assert themselves too strongly, we are enabled to perceive that experience is not, and never can be, a simple *duality*, consisting of subject and object only; but that in all experience there is present a third element, or aspect, or term. In other words a *knower* and a *thing known* imply *knowledge* (*logos*): *perceivers* and *objects perceived* imply *perceptions*: *actors* and *things acted upon* imply *actions*. In all experiences these three terms must necessarily co-exist; and inasmuch as each term bears a determinative relation to the other two, any attempt to dissociate them, to treat any one or two of them as though they could exist apart independently, must lead to error. The slightest change in one term implies a change in all. Thus a sequence of experiences, in course of time, involves a respective modification in these three variables.

When we speak of a series of "events" we make use of a customary convention which certainly suggests the fixity and independence of one element, the objective, in this trinity of experience. Similarly, when we speak of "facts" we refer to supposed actualities, circumstances, or events, considered as fixed entities complete in themselves. That this convention has great value as an expedient for our practical convenience, in view of the well-established polarization habits of thought, is undoubted.

It is evident no less from the conflict of testimony adduced in every lawsuit; from political, scientific and religious discussions; and from that aggregation of irreconcilable data, which is compiled in the name of "history," that the convention is not only fallible in its applications, but is productive of strife and confusion.

The fact is that the actual determination of one or of two elements of this trinity of experience, isolated from the rest, is not possible, any more than it is possible to make one or two straight lines enclose a space. It is this impossible task that the human personality is ever endeavouring to accomplish. One of the results of this endeavour is the evolution and multiplication of concepts or ideas in very great variety and complexity. As humanity is at present constituted the process of concept evolution is quite necessary, and within their proper sphere of activity these concepts, various and complex, are, of course, of very great practical utility; but for man's true mental development, their subordination to fundamental evolutionary processes, both in the individual and the race, is absolutely necessary.

The cramming of the individual mind with a large number of concepts, with their names, symbols and formulae, may result in the acquisition of a specific variety of intellectual efficiency related to that system of thought to which the concepts belong; but unless there is, at the same time, an awakening of some perception of the proper limitations of such a system and of its essentially relative nature, this mental cramming will be a hindrance rather than an assistance to higher intellectual growth.

Let us take, for example, one of the most important generalizations of modern science, namely that of *energy*. Energy is said to manifest itself as light, heat, mechanical work, chemical affinity, electricity, etc. Energy manifested in one form can be transmuted into its equivalent in another form and then back again into its original condition without loss. The transmission of force in railway locomotion will serve to illustrate the theory of conversion and conservation of energy. The potential chemical

affinity of the fuel burned in the furnace of the engine is converted into heat. Part of this liberated heat energy is dissipated
by conduction and radiation, but is all scientifically accounted
for. The remainder of the heat energy is converted into mechanical
work through the expansive force of steam. This mechanical
work is expended in overcoming the inertia and friction of the
moving mass, and at times also in overcoming the force of
gravity. Ultimately, through the resistances of friction and of
"concussion," the energy of mechanical motion is re-converted
into heat.

From the restricted point of view of physical science, energy
is constant, unchanged and unchangeable. From the point of
view of psycho-physics, nothing remains the same, and all the
modification in the manifestations of energy is determined by
the directive powers of mind. Thus in the illustration above cited
this directive power is, in great measure, our corporate intellectual
life; and quite obviously it is of material importance that the
mechanical energy of the moving mass should be systematically
re-converted into heat through the agency of brakes, rather than
through the more irregular mode of a collision.

The directive and co-ordinating powers of mind, in the determination of the manifestations of energy, vary according to the
varying forms in which life's processes are organised. Thus, in
the functioning of the human organism and of animal organisms
generally (viewing these primarily as vital organisms), the
directive powers take the form of conscious, subconscious, or
unconscious activities, usually in combination. In the functioning
of vegetable life they are for the most part unconscious, but also
collectively subconscious, using this term in its broadest signification; while in the mineral kingdom the directive powers, though
still *mind*, are strictly unconscious. (See note 4, p. 4, Chapter I.)

We come, therefore, to the conclusion that there is a great
multiplicity of "environments"; and that these exist not wholly
apart from and independently of psychic phases, but as comple-

mentary to them, in *their* multiplicity. Further, the awakening of our higher powers of synthetic understanding enables us to perceive that through their fluctuations and mutations all psycho-physical phases, whether we regard them in the light of "environments," states of "consciousness," "subconsciousness," "unconsciousness," or of "concepts," are necessarily correlated and interdependent, and are, without exception, subject to the reign of universal laws. Hence education in essence and purpose becomes an individualised process of discovering these laws, of finding their proper interpretation in the art of living and giving them synthetic expression in the growth of character.

CHAPTER VII

RELIGIONS, IDEALS, THE TWICE-BORN

FEW subjects present greater difficulties to the art of definition than those arising out of the confused maze of conflicting ideas, customs and traditions associated with the word "religion."

To say that religion is the sphere of human thought and practice, which pertains to the unmanifest side of individual and communal life, or what is usually termed the region of the "unseen," does not really carry us very far. Religion does more, it brings us in contact with those deep and intense convictions in the mind of man which have impelling forces greater in their scope and more enduring in their effects than those which arise out of physical conditions alone. These convictions are of various kinds and they impel men in different directions. They unite men into groups, they divide groups into sections, and they isolate individuals one from another. Religions, religious institutions and sects are almost innumerable. Their existence is based upon an immense variety of seemingly incompatible traditions, customs and creeds, which in their turn are associated with all kinds of human passions—good, bad and indifferent. Further, there is no fixity in religious systems. Like physical organisms they grow in strength to fruition and then decay. One religion appears to spring from another, or its life may be enriched or impoverished by the assimilation of ideas and influences derived from several sources simultaneously.

Notwithstanding all the confusion and perplexities which surround the subject, it is possible to discern, underlying the religious history of mankind, certain clear conceptions of priceless value; conceptions as to the aims, purposes and destiny of human life;

conceptions determining the emotions, conduct and language of individuals and races. All such conceptions belong properly to the domain of psychology.

It may be confidently asserted that practically every individual has at some time or another undergone distinct religious experiences—experiences, that is to say, which exalt the mind to a state of ecstasy; and whether it be the ecstasy of awe, of hope, or of rapture, such states of mind indicate for the individual his partial awakening to a perception of the real meaning of the existence to which he has been born. With the great majority of individuals such experiences are so rare and fleeting that they cannot be recalled as definite memories, but they nevertheless make some modification in the character.

William James, in that illuminating work *Varieties of Religious Experience*, has shown that there is a great similarity in the essence of these experiences, as distinguished from the mode of their separate occurrence. He contended that, in many cases, the intellectual capacity of the individuals who have these experiences is not adequate to a full and proper interpretation of their meaning; and that even when they are understood, the understanding is very rarely accompanied by the power to give such expression to their meaning in words as would carry conviction to the minds of others. Yet there is an abundance of evidence adduced, making it perfectly clear that many of the experiences belong to the same order; and that they must have been very real indeed to those who underwent them.

Several cases are cited in which a great mental revulsion takes place, a revulsion amounting to "conversion" or "change of heart." In those so converted the whole personal outlook seems to be radically altered; interests, tastes, aims and habits are transformed; the most intimate disposition appears to be fundamentally modified and renewed; the narrow and short-sighted self-interest, which actuated the previous life, gives place to higher human interests; the love of pleasure and gain yields to the love of truth,

P   5 or, as they generally prefer to express it, to the love of God; lust, anger and pride are subdued, while the individual energies so liberated find expression in benevolent activities. But, as William James points out, these changes of character are often neither so sudden nor so radical as they appear to be.

It will be remembered that, in the first chapter, personality was compared to an iceberg. Now an iceberg, unless it happens to be stranded, is a great mass of floating ice of which a small fraction only can be seen above the surface of the water. Ordinarily speaking, we depend upon our physical powers of vision in order to determine the size, shape and position of these very formidable obstacles to safe navigation. How unreliable this dependence upon mere eyesight can be we have learnt at severe cost.

The floating mass is continually shifting its centre of gravity. Occasionally, therefore, it happens that suddenly the visible portion disappears from view, and another portion, or it may be several portions simultaneously, emerges from invisible depths. Similarly what might be described as the centre of force in one's personality is subject, on occasion, to rapid and momentous changes of position in relation to the correlated system of complexes out of which the personality is composed. It is just these sudden changes in the centre of force which are often spoken of as "conversion." Those portions of personality emerging from the subconscious in our altered condition are not, in fact, newly created entities, they are merely transposed, and thus, for the time being, rendered dominant. What is more, the new position may resemble one of "unstable equilibrium," and it even suggests, to those who take a too rigid view of a fixed hypothetical self, a want of genuineness in the conversion. A careful investigation of a large number of cases led William James to the conclusion nevertheless that simulation was not the true explanation of the changed life which followed upon conversion.

The true explanation is briefly this: certain ideas, corresponding to what may be called the religious beliefs of others, are assimilated intellectually by an individual. These ideas become familiar, in a kind of unattached irresponsive manner, to a group of complexes which, linked together for practical purposes, constitute the normal waking personality; but the emotions properly associated with these ideas belong to another group of complexes which are, for the time being, subconscious, or latent; and to this group they gravitate and with it they coalesce. This process continues until this latter group has gained sufficient inherent strength, aided perhaps by some special outward circumstances, to force its emergence into vivid consciousness.

It is obvious that such spasmodic conversions have their drawbacks; and that the steady persistent growth of high character is far preferable. If one might venture upon an extension of the iceberg simile, a permanent change of heart would be comparable to the actual melting of the ice itself, so that its waters may combine freely with the waters of the ocean.

This last suggestion brings us to a point of great importance, namely, the extremely limited value of all imagery, and the great danger involved in dwelling upon a supposed analogy, which, though it may offer some passing help in the effective expression of an idea, cannot be properly regarded as the only symbol conveying that idea, or true for all time. More especially is this the case when we are endeavouring to explain some aspect of a process deep and far-reaching as is the growth and evolution of human individuality.

Images, phrases and formulas, which have been either invented or evolved for the purpose of conveying great truths, are undoubtedly quite necessary as educational instruments. But the inveterate tendency of the human mind to dwell needlessly upon such instruments inverts their proper relation in thought to the truths they are intended to teach; and hence there arise all the evils of dogmatism and idolatry. A well-made scaffolding, erected upon a sound system, is a useful contrivance for enabling us to build a great edifice, but if we forget the purpose for which the

scaffolding was contrived and so erect it that its subsequent removal would endanger the stability of the edifice itself, it will
readily be seen that it was not fulfilling its proper function. The
application of this principle to education may not be quite so
obvious, but it can hardly be less important. Creeds, conventions
and traditions, by long use and familiarity, breed in the mind of
man egoistic affections and attachments. These, with their re-
stricting influence upon perception and volition, bar the way to
spiritual growth and understanding. In this way the vehicles,
instruments, servants and friends, created by man for his higher
purposes and ends, tend to become his most formidable obstacles
and his deadliest foes.

What is a true ideal? Can it exist apart from the vehicle
through which it finds access to the human mind? This is a
difficult metaphysical problem and it is not necessary to solve it
here. But perhaps the best way of dealing with it is to show that
practically the same ideal may be found embodied in a great
variety of different dresses and shapes. This is the province of
comparative religion and philosophy; and already much excellent
educational work has been done in its fields.

In the framing of ideals, and in order to make sure that they
are really true and likely to be helpful towards furthering the
perfection of mankind, it is important, in the first place, to form
some clear conceptions as to the goal towards which humanity
is tending. As to this, there seem to be prevalent two sets of
ideals opposed the one to the other. In both human happiness is
the goal. According to one set of ideals the world is to be made
a better place to live in. Our notions of what is good for us are
to be accepted as practically fixed; circumstances and conditions
are to be adjusted to suit them. According to the opposite set of
ideals we must take the world as it is, call it "Nature" and adapt
our tastes and notions to suit it. It will be surmised from a
perusal of the preceding pages that, according to the psycho-
physical view, both sets of ideals are equally fallacious. Happiness

can only be real and lasting when we have entirely overcome that grasping attitude of mind which seeks to fix either mental disposition or environment as being capable of maintaining respectively permanent independence apart from one another.

It is the conquest of this grasping disposition of heart and mind which is the true meaning and implication of the process of being "born again in the spirit." All ideals conducing towards the attainment of this blessed state are, therefore, from a religious point of view, worthy and noble; all others are false and misleading.

Further, the *way* or *path* towards the attainment of this state, though accompanied by higher instinctive efforts, is essentially a *rational* way, using the term "rational" in contradistinction to mere intellectualism based upon the formation and arrangement of concepts. It is thus a process of rationalising instincts, subordinating those of reproduction and preservation to those innate spiritual tendencies which make for human perfection or wholeness. Mere devotion to noble ideals is not sufficient. New and keener mental powers and faculties must be developed and maintained. Mere repression is useless. No part of our nature can be ignored in the spiritual process. The lower instincts have to be *sublimated*, not denied. The errors which arise from complex dissociations, however slight, must be overcome, the perverted beliefs and cravings engendered by such dissociations, the false notions of fixity, permanence and universality in the concepts obtaining in such complexes must all be re-coordinated or resolved. The emotions allied to the minor and intermediate complexes must be purified and exalted and their energies redirected, so that they can find outlet and expression in harmony with the growth of the Great Complex. Unless this is thoroughly accepted and understood, the individual can never gain any lasting confidence and security. The process is called painful, but although it is true that great suffering is involved, the pain which has to be endured is more than counterbalanced by the joy of achievement, and is ever diminishing in intensity.

In our efforts towards perfection there must be true self-examination; not mere intellectual introspection. The recorded wisdom of our predecessors, and that of contemporary thinkers, are certainly of some avail, but each individual must rely chiefly upon his own inward efforts to break that crusted mass of ignorance, preconception and prejudice which we all inherit. If in the end one finds that these efforts and the glorified traditions of the past are really identical in purpose, the actual discovery of this identity and the realization of its truth are part of the process which each individual must necessarily undergo for himself.

Then can we not help one another? Yes, surely. As William James points out in his *Varieties of Religious Experience*, the practice of "confession" may have very great value psychologically, provided the confessor has a large and well-equipped mind. He should be thoroughly well versed in psychology, and he should be possessed of more than an average knowledge of the affairs of the world. He should also be sincere, kind-hearted, disinterested and, above all, he should be endowed with a large fund of common sense. The "professional"[1] confessor is rarely so equipped, and, consequently, the operation in his hands may be worse than useless.

It often happens, at the present time, that those in trouble fall back on the doctor or the lawyer for advice and guidance. Is it too much to hope that some day, in the distant future, the properly qualified doctor, surgeon, lawyer and teacher may each and all of them combine in themselves the highest functions of both priest and healer?

Careless or unskilled discussions may sometimes have the

---

[1] The word *professional* is ambiguous. Its use above implies the presence of the commercial element, i.e., work done for a "consideration," or an occupation in pursuit of a "living." William James contrasts professional work with that of the amateur, as involving in the former case greater regard to *method* and in the latter case a regard mainly to *results*. The suggestion in the text is that proficiency in both these respects is dependent upon knowledge and upon untrammelled beneficence.

effect of awakening the Great Complex, the whole personality; especially if it has been awakened before, or even if it has previously been on the verge of an awakening. More often such discussions, when they effect a change in the point of view, have merely been instrumental in altering the field of consciousness by bringing another unimportant complex into the focus of awareness.

As indicated in Chapter iv, great importance attaches to the development of higher incentives to effort. How often we repeat or refer to the "Sermon on the Mount," and pay lip service to its beauty and its truth! But what is its true meaning? "A counsel of perfection" is the glib official reply. Certainly, but has it no practical value, and, if so, what is it intended to convey? Restated in cold prosaic language, the lesson there inculcated urges us to rely less upon the seen, the concrete, the physically tangible; and more upon the spiritual side of our natures, unmanifest to our senses, but none the less real and permanent. We are there told on authority that by this way we gain true security and everlasting peace.

That this teaching is in strict accord with the conclusions of recent psychological research, it is one of the objects of these pages to point out.

CHAPTER VIII

INVERSION

THE process of *inversion*, which reverses, distorts and confuses our relations and interests in the conduct of life, has already been alluded to several times. It is usually spoken of as a psychological process, but more correctly, it is *psycho-physiological* because there is necessarily a somatic aspect to be considered.

It is proposed in this chapter to deal with the matter more exhaustively, with a view to explaining how it arises, and how it can be avoided, except, of course, where the process is beneficent.

In discussions of our inverted mental conditions, there is often much vehement disputation as to whether they should be treated physiologically or psychologically, or both physiologically and psychologically. The answer to this question depends mainly on the specific kind of mental condition we have under consideration. There are, for example, several kinds of inversion. Inversions do not necessarily imply disorders of the mind. They may be both malignant and beneficent, according to circumstances, and they may take place suddenly or gradually. The "conversions" dealt with in the last chapter exemplify rapid inversions in relation to religious beliefs; and they may be looked upon as being, on the whole, beneficent. Illustrations are so numerous and various that we must confine ourselves to a few typical examples. A good illustration of an invariable functional inversion, at once gradual and beneficent, is afforded by the mental transposition of images cast by light rays upon the retina of the eye. The optical pictures falling on the retina are, of course, upside down. Spontaneously and automatically our minds make these inverted pictures appear right side up in our perceptions. It is not difficult to understand why this should be so. The persistent wish to avoid the inconvenience of seeing everything upside down, and having to make a conscious effort to interpret our perceptions correctly, brings about an automatic mental adjustment.

In this case it is clearly the strong wish which is the determinative cause of the inversion. We have seen that wishes determine beliefs; and that wishes, in combination with a system of ideas linked together with certain memories and actions in specific experiences, are the origin of complexes. If now a complex is actuated by so potent a wish or emotion, that it gains a dominant influence in our lives, it will thus bring about a personal outlook the reverse of that determined by other complexes less potently actuated. In this way, a complex, or a group of complexes, dissociated from the rest by fixed ideas, may establish an inversion of the more normal beliefs held by a person (or an association of persons) in regard to any specific subject.

There is a form of mania known as "hysterical anorexy," which consists chiefly in a systematic refusal of food. Charcot attributed this disease to the dominance of fixed ideas. The following case is famous from his repeated reference to it in his writings: while undressing a patient of this kind, he found that she wore round her waist a rose-coloured ribbon. Charcot obtained from the patient this confidence, that the ribbon was a measure her waist must not exceed. She had said to him: "I prefer dying of hunger to becoming big as mamma." Janet referring to this case says: "Coquetries of this kind are very frequent, one of my patients refused to eat for fear that during her digestion her face should grow red and appear less pleasant in the eyes of a professor whose lectures she attended after her meals."

Such cases, which are very numerous, illustrate specific inversions, arising out of some trifling mental obsession. A strong wish to gain some personal end grows and develops until it becomes dominant in the personality; and any means towards that end, presenting itself persistently in thought, as being all-

important, becomes an obsession; until at last this *means* usurps
the position and authority of the original *end*. Hence the inversion. Miserliness is another familiar example. Wealth is
regarded as the highest good. The acquisition and preservation
of property are, therefore, aimed at as the supreme end and aim of
existence. Money as the symbol of wealth, the instrument of its
exchange and the measure of its value, is sought after, and prized.
The next step is to regard money as constituting in itself the *end*.

William James, in *Varieties of Religious Experience*, cites a
remarkable case of inversion and miserliness. A young man of
large fortune, but not over-burdened with brains, had an extremely generous disposition. He trusted everybody. Consequently he had a large number of "friends," who flattered,
deceived and cheated him. The result was that he soon lost the
whole of his fortune, and was reduced to dire penury. Naturally
his friends deserted him. One day, meditating on his forlorn
position, he swore a solemn oath that he would recover his whole
fortune, or build up a larger one. He at once set to work. He
gained a few pennies by holding horses and doing odd jobs. He
lived most frugally, invested his savings with great care and
judgment; and in the course of a few years he amassed an enormous fortune, far larger than the one he originally possessed, and
died a hopelessly wretched miser.

Inversions are far more serious in their consequences when
they are not merely personal, but infect large masses of the
population, as they are apt to do in the world of economics.
Thus we become witnesses to-day of very strange spectacles.
Great sections of a community are enthusiastically united on the
preposterous creed that true welfare and commercial prosperity
can be secured by no other means than by creating an artificial
scarcity of things in general demand. It is true that the particular
scarcity insisted upon varies with the special "interests" of
different sections. We are assured in one direction that it is a
specific "line of goods" that most needs rarefying, in another
direction we hear that the important matter is that "labour"

should be scarce, in another it is professional services, and so on. The reason given is, that the holders of these commodities would thereby be able to obtain better prices for their wares. In this manner there would be more money available to go round, and we should all be made happier. Now several nations, notably Germany, have tried this method in practice. It can be confidently stated that, never since history began to be recorded, has any people ever had at its disposal such enormous quantities of money as present-day Germany. So great, indeed, is the abundance there, that the unit of exchange is no less than a billion marks; and practically every individual in the country is a billionaire. This is a drastic way of curing a people of their folly. One can only hope it will be effective.

The unintelligent use of symbols, analogies, emblems and allegories supplies us, in every-day life, with an endless variety of inversions. Inversions of this type begin so subtly to work their way upon the character, that it is often difficult to trace their effects upon our manner of thinking, until they have become ridiculous, invidious and markedly pronounced. They are, perhaps, the greatest enemies of clear thought. They all follow the same general process in their development. One becomes enamoured of some phrase or figure of speech, expressive of a supposed analogy or illustration; and by constant repetition, it seems to grow in authority, until one comes at last to believe that it supplies in itself a conclusive argument for almost any purpose, even though to others it may appear wholly irrelevant.

It is the same with *conventions*, but in this case inversions are generally more infectious. Inverted conventions are, indeed, so numerous that the word "conventional" has come to mean, colloquially, nothing more than dependence on some useless, meaningless, or obsolete notion. Yet, as a fact, convention and symbolism correctly understood are essential factors in all speech, conduct, and general thought. The importance, therefore, of being constantly on our guard against the development of harmful inversions can hardly be overestimated.

CHAPTER IX

PERFECTION AS THE IDEAL AND LESSONS OF THE WAR

ERFECTION is the highest ideal, the ultimate goal. Although colloquially it is often an appreciative expression merely, or a mere mark of high approbation, needless to say that perfection means properly a condition of things which can by no possibility be improved upon. In its true sense perfection is rarely thought of seriously as a practical ideal, much less is it to be met with in actual life. Applied to human personality it implies not only excellence of quality, but absolute completeness as to individual development and capacity in every respect. It implies complete knowledge, which is indistinguishable from complete faith, for no incomplete knowing or believing can ever be perfect knowledge or belief. It implies complete power, in that a perfect individual would never try to do or have the least wish to do anything that he was unable to accomplish. It implies absolute sincerity, for perfection is altogether incompatible with untruthfulness or any effort to deceive. It implies unlimited patience, for there could be with perfection neither false expectations nor the desire to obtain results before they are properly due. In the same way it implies absolute kindness, wisdom and understanding.

All this is fairly obvious and mainly matter of verbal definition; yet how often do we hear men blamed because in certain respects they have fallen short of perfection. The fact is that most of us are much too fond of setting up impossible standards or at least of imposing arbitrary and impracticable ideals for the regulation of one another's conduct.

We have dealt in a previous chapter with "reality" and "fact," but the use of these words has an important bearing on the present issue. We have seen that "reality" and "fact" are often mere question-begging terms purporting to fix some permanent value to phenomena; and that, except within specific systems involving definite preconceptions as to what is or is not manifest through the senses, this use of the words has not even the excuse of convenience. The only true facts pertaining to the ideal are the laws of individual existence. The estimation of ideals cannot, therefore, be dealt with according to strictly inductive methods of reasoning. The ordinary laws of evidence and proof are not applicable to the determination of their value, except in so far as they may help towards their verification and elucidation. Ideals are based primarily upon insight and intuition.

The pursuit of perfection requires, undoubtedly, the tentative formulation of noble ideals, that is to say of those crystalline glimpses of the direction in which the true goal lies; but the danger of all such formulations is that they are apt to be mistaken for the goal itself.

The Great War has been to a world, striving indeed for the most part to do what is right, a profound revelation of the vast extent of human imperfection. This is the chief lesson to be learned from the War, and one that must be learned thoroughly before we can hope to arrive at any sound estimate of the outcome of this world-wide strife, or find the solutions of the vexed problems of fixing its causes and determining the burden of ultimate responsibility. In our examinations of such questions few have learned as yet how to distinguish what is essential from what is not essential, or how to avoid the confusion of one with the other. This confusion is not merely verbal, or one of mere technical definition. It is fundamental, and gives rise to much bitter controversy on questions of methods and ideals. Thus we find that there are different, not to say diametrically opposed, ways by which the striking events of life may be considered. They may be considered superficially, or as we often say "practically," from the point of view of materialistic habits of thought, or else they may be considered with a view to the deeper spiritual aspects of life. There is also the middle course; where events are examined simultaneously from both points of view in their proper relationship and true perspective. In the Buddhist scriptures a story is related of how a dying father told his son to avoid looking at things "either from too far or too near": wise advice, much neglected at the present time.

Let us endeavour to examine the problem of the responsibility for the War from all these aspects. First let us try to define what we mean by a state of war. Similes taken from natural phenomena may be helpful. The surface of the earth is continually changing by processes known to the student of physical and biological sciences, but, except for the ordinary seasonal changes, the alterations in the conformation and composition of the earth's crust are so gradual as to suggest to uninstructed observers the appearance of fixity and permanence. Occasionally, however, it happens that the cumulative effects of pent-up energies, breaking loose from a state of unstable equilibrium, produce such violent and sudden rearrangements in the outward conformation and condition of visible things as to give rise to a belief in the operation of entirely new and unforeseeable agencies. Among such exceptional phenomena are storms, floods, land-slides, earthquakes, volcanic eruptions and epidemics. In the light of modern science, however, no greater mystery surrounds these exceptional occurrences than that which accompanies normal life in the mind of enlightened and thoughtful people.

So it is with the outbreak of war.

Civil law, through which we manage and regulate our collective relationships in times of peace, is based upon the expectation of a more or less continuous flow of the petty forces of our social and industrial activities. At best it is but the embodiment of some rough generalizations as to the way in which our established customs and beliefs should or are supposed to operate in the ordinary life of a community. It is true that of recent years there has grown up a body of thought styled "international law," intended to govern a theoretical community of all nations. Great as may be the promise and hope founded upon this legal growth of thought, it can hardly be said, as yet, to have emerged from its elementary stages, and its serious students are few and far between. Now the civil law of a nation, although modified and adjusted by periodic acts of legislation, and changing also through desuetude in the lapse of time, can never be properly described as a perfect expression or mirror of the actual needs, feelings and aspirations of a progressive people. This being the case, all nations are confronted from time to time with manifestations of sectional discontent, culminating in revolt, with greater or less violence and frequency, according to the wisdom of rulers, the elasticity of legal provisions and the character and resourcefulness of the people. It is not surprising, therefore, to find wide differences, even of a fundamental nature, in the civil law of various nations. These differences depend not only upon the geographical, climatic, political and religious conditions of their respective populations, but on their temperamental qualities, whether active or latent.

These differences in the character and conditions of nations are of course liable to clash through the operations of opposing political interests and trade rivalries; and when such clashing occurs, appeal is, in the first instance, made to the nebulous provisions of international law. But, as already indicated, its provisions are often inadequate. The reason of this inadequacy is really not far to seek. The study of psychology gives us a clue. As humanity is constituted the emotional qualities of mind, i.e., our likes and dislikes, our interests and cravings, determine, in great measure, our beliefs, opinions and "convictions" as to what is right and what is true. This applies not only to individuals, but to groups, or combinations of individuals, united for a common purpose. A national crisis invariably tends to bring about unity within the nation of its interests and convictions. This unity in crises is a strange conglomeration of panic, pride, ill-will and national enthusiasm, which passes, for want of a better word, as "patriotism." Failure in the adjustment of differences between nations through diplomatic appeals to international law precipitates a state of war.

All impartial observers of the present world-crisis are agreed that Great Britain, loyally supported by France, Russia, Serbia and Italy, made most determined and persistent appeals, through proper diplomatic channels, to international law in its endeavours to bring about a peaceful solution, or failing that, some provisional adjustment which would give opportunity and scope to the healing operations of time. That this is a correct diagnosis is supported by the practically unanimous attitude of sympathy shown by all neutral Powers, as well as that of the British and the Allies' dominions and colonial dependencies throughout the world.

With the outbreak of war every belligerent nation goes through a remarkable transformation. Whatever may be the case, *theoretically*, in times of peace, at the first signs of war the whole population becomes suddenly awakened to the supremacy of the State. Civil law is in many ways superseded by martial law. The Government assumes new powers, a widened and more arbitrary authority. In our case Parliament has sanctioned the enactment of new laws, valid for the duration of the War, which modify in the most fundamental manner personal rights, the rights of property and the liberty of speech. These laws were passed without delay, without opposition, and practically without discussion! The changes wrought by the War in the condition of Great Britain were far more dramatic and spectacular than those which took place in Germany and Austria, particularly the former. For in Prussianised Germany, where military and autocratic rule has always been more or less normal, the ideals and methods of government during peace are widely different from our own. This fact brings us close to the main issues of responsibility. The dominant governing power and authority in Germany was in the hands of what is called "Prussian Junkerdom." It is the rule of an aristocratic and military caste. Its ideal is the supremacy of, and reverence for, physical force. It involves the organised subordination of individual rights and interests to the supposed needs of the State, as determined by privileged classes, social and economic. With us the State is the synthetic expression of the considered aims and wishes of the whole community. If the Government of the day fails to give adequate expression to this synthesis, it is changed. Our constitution may be far from perfect in its practical working, but that, at any rate, is the ideal which animates it. Public opinion with us is a real force, the ultimate determining power; but in the former German Empire public opinion must either conform to an arbitrary Government authority or be suppressed. It is not, of course, to be assumed that Germany had an absolute monopoly of the Prussian Junkerdom spirit: for indeed that spirit is to be found widely distributed throughout the world. Many individuals everywhere, and many communities, pass through phases of its baneful influence. It does not follow, however, that because that spirit is to be seen active, or its latent existence felt, it need always prevail and dominate; nor is it true, as often suggested, that anyone is necessarily hypocritical for the reason that, while he is himself tainted with its virus, he, at the same time, repudiates it as an *ideal*. Here then, possibly, we have a solution of the problem of responsibility. The German nation was so much imbued with the lust of dominion and the belief in its own superiority that it could not, as a nation, co-operate amicably with other nations, granting to all a share of what it claimed for itself.

It is to be hoped that this appalling War, with all its horrible devastation, will at least have this good to its credit, that it will result in the subjugation, if not the final laying, of that pestilent spirit of physical dominion and avarice for many a long year to come.

Let us, however, avoid as far as we can falling into the grave error of self-righteousness—of becoming too complaisant and optimistic. Wherever one looks, human nature, in its existing stages of development, is very far from perfect, and, recognising this fact, let us avoid all unnecessary harshness of criticism—that pernicious habit of hastily forming arrogant judgments, based upon a superficial survey of outward events. "Ideals" we all have, but few of them are worthy of being lived up to, and many of us have from time to time a jumble of conflicting "ideals," both true and false. It is easy enough to find fault, for while an "ideal" holds us, our emotional natures blind us not only to our own shortcomings but to the relatively true value of other "ideals" with which we happen for the time being to be out of sympathy. We often pride ourselves on our "consistency," but who is there truly consistent other than the absolutely perfect man? Some are apt to forget, too, that it is better to be inconsistent, with occasional lapses into virtue and modesty, than to be consistent in the determined pursuit of false ideals.

CHAPTER X

SUMMARY

In dealing with *purpose* as a fundamental issue in education, as in other matters, it is often asked: where and what is the supreme *authority*, or the *sanction*, on which purpose depends, and by which it is directed? The answer to this question, which has been propounded in these pages, is that true authority must be looked for within, and that ultimately it is there that it will be found.

The acknowledgement and acceptance by an individual, or by a group of individuals, of any externally constituted authority, must imply an inward assent on the part of the individual or group, otherwise the acknowledgement itself would not be genuine. Hence it follows that whatever procedure may be adopted for bringing authority home, the sanction must, in the end, be indwelling not external. That a false outward authority may prevail for a time is, of course, well recognised, but sooner or later it is dissipated and overthrown, which outcome is the mark of its falsity.

The word "conscience," although at times much abused, has held by long tradition the implication of that indwelling mentor, supreme and infallible in its authority and power for the preservation of the human race. Numerous familiar terms, e.g., reason, understanding, insight, intuition and the like, could be called into service for the same purpose, though it is true they all savour of question-begging. A man is not necessarily rational because he calls himself a "rationalist," nor gifted with insight because he is called a "seer"; but there is a quality of the human mind nearly everyone unites in praising, a quality which we are exhorted as a duty to exercise, namely *toleration* or *impartiality*. In spite of

6–2

the admonition to respect this quality, it is indeed rather rare, for it implies an unprejudiced apprehension of the true. Impartiality implies, not indifference or apathy, but the subjugation of our egoism.

The explanations and illustrations of this process of subjugation need not be elaborated here, but it will be remembered that the doctrine inculcated is that, through the relinquishment and ultimate dissolution of personal egoism, in other words through self-conquest, there is developed in the mind the powers of clear insight and true understanding. That is to say, over-emotional or conflicting wishes obscure true vision and create delusions; while harmonious motives bring about freedom of thought, elasticity of expression, efficiency and capacity in action, not only in ourselves, but by sympathetic infection, in our fellows also. This way leads to mutual understanding and genuine friendship. It is the true solvent of dissension and strife. The foolish may exclaim that this kind of existence would make life very dull. It would not. Dullness springs from restlessness, stupidity, lack of resource, and nervous exhaustion. Harmonious motives prevent waste of vital energy. Harmony liberates energy for productive purposes, and makes the mind keen in the pursuit of its own healthful development, including necessarily the minds of our fellows, seeing that our individual lives are in essence interdependent.

Short-sighted pleasure-seeking, as a predominant ideal, inevitably leads to disappointment and pessimism, inasmuch as the pleasures sought compete with one another in their claims for attention, and can never be completely satisfied.

The belief that "we were meant to be happy," irrespective of all evidence to the contrary, is a delusion deeply implanted in our natures. In practice this delusion takes the form of insisting that we have a prescriptive right to the gratification of all our ephemeral wants. Absurd as this claim appears in the light of experience, it is in practice an awkward matter to deal with, for there is a half-truth underlying it, the repudiation of which appears like sheer cruelty. If instead of postulating the incongruity that "we were meant to be happy," we were to say that we all should, as in duty bound, learn how to become truly happy, we would be nearer the mark; and indeed this amended postulate supplies us in a nutshell with a serviceable formula for the *purpose of education.*

APPENDIX

NOTE ON DETERMINISM

In an appendix to the two previous issues of the *Purpose of Education*, various comments of reviewers and correspondents were quoted together with short replies either of acknowledgement or correction. The most important of these comments were from the pen of Dr John Adams. He asked for further elucidation on points. Particularly he wished to know the relation of the psycho-physical system propounded in these pages with Freudianism and psychological "determinism." In the first chapter of this new edition "psycho-analysis" has been dealt with more fully than was attempted in the former appendices; while *determinism*, although not specifically referred to as a system of thought, is touched upon in Chapter VI. It may, however, be pointed out here that "determinism" is ambiguous in that it at the same time insists that conscious volition is a delusion, and yet admits delusion as an important determinative factor in causation. It is of course obvious that psychological phenomena, such as "motives" and their effects, must be acknowledged to be interdependent and correlated, but that does not imply that the sequence of all phenomena is absolutely fixed and invariable. One must recognise the distinction between cause and occasion. The doctrine that we are all involved, with everything else in Nature, in an absolutely fixed, necessary and unalterable course of "objective" events, is not only false but logically unmeaning.

Briefly stated, psycho-physical biology is an expression of the spatial and chronological aspects of phenomenal relations. These relations, far from being absolutely determinate, become less exact and measurable (in the spatial and chronological senses) as *mind*

becomes less differentiated in its upward growth towards what
has been called the Great Complex. Freudians invariably use
the word "complex" in a pathological sense. This has led to
some confusion. The use made of the word in this book is not
by any means new. Professor Rhys Davids employed the word
"complex" more than 40 years ago to translate certain Buddhist
philosophical terms, long before Freudianism was ever heard of.

The former dogmatic attitude of distinguished men of science
is rapidly disappearing with the great expansion which is taking
place in the fields of experimental research. Thus we find to-day,
more especially in France, many able investigators into the
region of "super-normal" phenomena; that is to say of phenomena
not generally believed to be within the true scope of exact
experimental methods. Various scientific writers of great emin-
ence could be cited, but as these do not as yet represent a body
of thinkers who have any clear or agreed doctrine to expound,
it is not necessary to refer to them specifically. There is, however,
an excellent summary of what the best scientific work in this
sphere has done in recent times. *Supernormal Faculties in Man
—an Experimental Study*, by Dr Eugène Osty, translated from
the French by Stanley De Brath, M.Inst.C.E. (Methuen), can
be confidently recommended. This work is a conscious and
painstaking analysis of a vast mass of evidence compiled and
critically examined by a well-known practitioner in nervous
pathology.

INDEX

For EU product safety concerns, contact us at Calle de José Abascal, 56–1°, 28003 Madrid, Spain or eugpsr@cambridge.org.

 www.ingramcontent.com/pod-product-compliance
Ingram Content Group UK Ltd.
Pitfield, Milton Keynes, MK11 3LW, UK
UKHW012333130625
459647UK00009B/257